C000003039

'This is a compelling read; a boc
stories Eva recounts from her own life and from the lives of others are often
heartbreakingly sad – but her focus isn't on the heartbreak but on the hope
and encouragement which she has gleaned from a life soaked in the truth
of scripture.'
Mags Duggan, author, retreat leader and speaker

'This book is an easy read yet rich with insights, comfort and encouragement
– a must for anyone who seeks healing and desires to experience God afresh.'
Anissa Chung, UKCP registered psychotherapist and supervisor

'*This Crown of Comfort* is the wondrous feast that God prepares for us in
the presence of our enemies. No matter how broken we are, God calls us to
come to him and receive and savour his love and care. A wonderful book
for women to read and study together.'
Lee Merrill Byrd, author, publisher and editor

'No matter how broken or hurt we are, we are given in this excellent book
the tools or 'the calls of God' to build a bridge to healing and wholeness.
This book reminds us of God's deep love for us in our time of greatest need
and provides a spiritual balm for every situation.'
Dawn Braithwaite, solicitor and consultant

'Eva provides readers with great insight to the very God of comfort that we
all so need – men and women. While written to women, this is a treasure
trove coming from the seven calls of God found in Isaiah.'
Don Pape, literary agent, Pape Commons

'Eva takes you on a valuable journey to see life's inexplicable and relentless
pains. There is much to linger over and explore along the way, in order to
gain new vistas and perspectives, that bring both life and hope.'
Fiona Oommen, business general manager and leadership coach

'This is a powerful and thought-provoking book to be read thoughtfully and
prayerfully for those who question how to live fruitfully through all that life
throws at them. Thank you, Eva, for sharing what God has done.'
Alison Jackson, retired GP

15 The Chambers, Vineyard
Abingdon OX14 3FE
brf.org.uk

Bible Reading Fellowship is a charity (233280)
and company limited by guarantee (301324),
registered in England and Wales

ISBN 978 1 80039 208 3
First published 2023
10 9 8 7 6 5 4 3 2 1 0
All rights reserved

Text © Eva Leaf 2023
This edition © Bible Reading Fellowship 2023
Cover illustration © Namosh/stock.adobe.com

The author asserts the moral right to be identified as the author of this work

Acknowledgements
Scripture quotations are taken from The Holy Bible, New International Version®,
NIV®. Copyright © 1973, 1978, 1984, 2011 by Biblica, Inc.™ Used by permission of
Zondervan. All rights reserved worldwide.

Most names and places have been changed.

Every effort has been made to trace and contact copyright owners for material
used in this resource. We apologise for any inadvertent omissions or errors, and
would ask those concerned to contact us so that full acknowledgement can be
made in the future.

A catalogue record for this book is available from the British Library

Printed and bound by CPI Group (UK) Ltd, Croydon CR0 4YY

THIS CROWN OF COMFORT

God's seven calls to women in distress

EVA LEAF

And provide for those who grieve in Zion – to bestow on them a crown of beauty instead of ashes, the oil of joy instead of mourning.
ISAIAH 61:3

To every generous person interviewed in this book,
thank you for sharing the deep things of your lives.

To everyone who read this book on its formative journey,
thank you for making it the richer.

CONTENTS

4 God's fourth call: depart!

5 God's fifth call: build up!

6 God's sixth call: pass through!

7 God's seventh call: build up!

Preface

For years I searched the Bible for those places where God spoke with women. I knew that Jesus related with many women in his time, and I clung on to his words, receiving them as if spoken to me. They brought me comfort and guided me. Yet I found very few God-to-woman conversations in the Old Testament. Had I missed something? Surely the heart of Jesus and God were entwined as one, and both deeply cared about us women.

One rainy holiday as my family and I hunkered down in our tent, I sat in my sleeping bag and flicked through the Bible. I started at chapter 1 of Genesis, the first book in the Bible, and then, 700 pages later, in the book of Isaiah, I finally found it. I read an outpouring of God's heart towards a city called Jerusalem. He called her a beloved woman!

My heart jumped as I read familiar passages, as if for the first time. I saw God's heart for women. I saw his tender response to our brokenness and sadness. And as I read, I discovered seven places where God called out to Jerusalem amid her tears, seven places where he repeated himself – his caring double imperatives.[1] He deeply loved her. He wanted her to find joy and hope. Then it occurred to me: those seven double imperatives had already been a part of my life for years, like seven jewels in a crown, encircling me with his grace.

God once again validated me. He confirmed his love for me as a woman, for I too had been broken like Jerusalem. And because I finally saw it in the book of Isaiah, it gave me courage to share it. Many of us women may still wonder if God loves us, if he cares deeply about what happens to us.

He does.

Introduction

We all have experienced troubles in one way or another. And even though each of our stories is different, we may all have prayed the same – for God to rescue us. I constantly did, especially as a young woman living in the USA, as I lived through homelessness, isolation and harsh treatment. Later in England and overseas as a Christian worker, I went through other troubles – loneliness and five miscarriages.

Thankfully for all of us, God sees the bigger picture. He answers our prayers, but he also comforts us and helps us grow strong. He enables us to move forward in life and overcome the heart consequences these troubles will cause.

In the book of Isaiah, God calls out seven double imperatives to a broken Jerusalem. She too experienced terrible times, but God didn't leave his beloved Jerusalem there. He didn't abandon her. Instead, his seven calls opened a way towards living in wholeness. They became like jewels in a crown on her head. For in Isaiah 61:3, God promises to 'provide for those who grieve in Zion – to bestow on them a crown of beauty instead of ashes, the oil of joy instead of mourning'. And as we stay close to him, we too can receive his crown of beauty, his comfort and restoration. For without a doubt, we too are his beloved.

The seven calls of God form the seven chapters in this book. To explore them more deeply, each chapter comes in two parts and includes a time for personal reflection.

- **Call 1 – Comfort!** God tenderly cries out to a hurting Jerusalem. And it is a tender call for each one of us, for his comfort is there for hurting hearts.

- **Call 2 – Awake! Rise up!** God shows Jerusalem what is going on in her life. And the same is true for us. For in order to heal, we must understand why we hurt.

- **Call 3 – Awake! Get dressed!** God lovingly provides Jerusalem with clothes to wear. And we too can accept them, putting on strength and courage.

- **Call 4 – Depart!** God earnestly desires for Jerusalem to leave behind everything which holds her back. And the same is true for us. We can't move on until we have let go.

- **Call 5 – Build up!** God called his beloved Jerusalem to himself, desiring a relationship with her. And we too can experience this by drawing close to him.

- **Call 6 – Pass through!** God gives Jerusalem the confidence to step back into the world, a new person. And he gives us the confidence to be our new selves.

- **Call 7 – Build up!** Like Jerusalem, God wants us to share his seven calls, enabling others to draw close to him. And as we do, our hearts will grow in confidence.

All the stories in this book are true, taken from interviews with other women, from my own life and from the Bible. Some are situations many of us may have experienced; others are extreme. Yet despite everything we go through, God's seven calls are relevant today. For in his tender love, he shows us our beauty and worth. In his powerful love, he gives us strength.

1

GOD'S FIRST CALL: COMFORT!

Comfort, comfort my people, says your God. Speak tenderly to Jerusalem.
Isaiah 40:1–2

A tender call to comfort a broken and hurting Jerusalem. And a tender call to each one of us. For comfort is only required when our hearts hurt.

God's comfort: am I worth it?

Comfort, comfort my people, says your God. Speak tenderly to Jerusalem.

My troubles seemed to settle after I set myself a goal – to get rid of every conflict and grief in my life. I had seen what troubles did to others and had experienced too many already in my growing-up years. So I came up with a plan and congratulated myself. But it turned out to be one of the biggest mistakes of my life.

What was this plan? I decided to agree with the disagreeable to avoid conflict. I conformed to what people demanded of me to foster peaceful relationships. I even determined to under-achieve, so as not to get noticed, for when I stood out, I became a target. It was a peace at all costs, so I could feel somewhat safe. But it didn't work out as I had hoped. As my teenage years rolled by, the consequences grew. By the time I reached adulthood, they broke me and spewed me out. Thankfully, God was there the entire time, collecting the pieces, waiting for me to ask for help. He had another plan for me.

I have talked with others who also shared stories of incredible heartbreak and trouble, some things they couldn't help in life and some things they could. Tragedy. Bereavement. Sickness. Abuse. Accusations. Betrayal. Mistakes. Yet many of those people had one thing in common – they dared to let God come close and help. They dared to accept his other plan. Sure, they acknowledged that they had changed as people, but here they gave a surprised smile. For even though they would never be able to turn back time, never be unhurt again, God did something extraordinary.

A few years back my husband, Derek, and I took our children to the States to celebrate our 25th wedding anniversary. While there, we came upon a real-life example of what trouble looks like in nature. We drove down Highway 40 in the Arizona desert and noticed a sign saying, 'Meteor Crater Road'. Out of curiosity, we turned off and drove out into what seemed like endless desert. What a surprise to find a crater, and even a visitors' centre.

The billboard out front said it was the best-preserved crater in the world, so we walked around the exhibition and read the facts. We marvelled that this meteor had travelled at an incredible 26,000 miles an hour when it slammed into earth! Apparently, it totally altered the place where it struck. We studied the diagrams, and I started scribbling down notes. This sounded too much like real life.

Then we gathered in a group at an appointed time and waited for a guide to take us up to the actual site. About 30 of us filed up, and I gasped in amazement. The hole spanned a mile across and sank down 500 feet. The ground had literally exploded on impact, and what had been on the inside ended up outside. Not only that, but the impact changed the constitution of the ground, searing it into pockmarked, glass-like rock. Now, tens of thousands of years later, I stood there in front of the evidence!

I stared at the gigantic hole, thinking this is exactly what happens. Metaphorical meteors strike us down and leave us sprawled on the floor. Each of us gets turned inside out and shocked into permanent change. My mind jumped back to my first major 'meteor strike'. I was 17, and only months before I graduated from high school, I was ordered to drop out due to a family situation. I had dreamed of becoming a doctor, not quitting and working in a menial job.

I remember standing in front of my bedroom mirror that awful day, getting changed from school clothes into work clothes. I stared at myself. No one would see the distress in my heart, that my dreams had just been hacked to pieces. My outside appearance lied to everyone around me, for physically I still looked well. I still had all my limbs, but I had been wounded and knocked over by a metaphorical meteor, one that altered the entire course of my life.

Strangely, it took years to grasp the depth of brokenness and the long-lasting effects of having tried to keep a false peace. When Derek and I got married, I hardly talked about my past. We lived in another country, I had new friends and no one other than Derek knew what had happened. I kept it a secret and I wanted to keep it that way. I thought I could simply forget, and it would leave no residual effect.

Then one day my own precious daughter turned 17, a beautiful, gentle, gracious young woman. And the locked door to my memories exploded open. I saw my own life in hers. I saw that my heart still hurt profoundly all those years later, and I wept in agony behind closed doors, sprawled on the floor once again. No amount of forgetting could change the fact that my troubles had altered me. I could never go back. I too had changed.

I reached for my Bible. Was there anything God could say that would wash away the pain? I doubted it. I couldn't change the past, and God wouldn't. It would always remain my history and could never be undone. But as I read, I finally understood; Jesus suffered meteor-sized troubles as well.

His enemies maligned him. They hurt and wounded him. They killed him. After his resurrection, Jesus told one of his disciples, 'Put your finger here; see my hands. Reach out your hand and put it into my side' (John 20:27). The traumas Jesus suffered had changed him as well. His scars, just like mine, were deep, and he would carry them throughout eternity.

I can't tell you how much this comforted me. If Jesus could accept and embrace his changes, so could I. If he could get up and keep on living, so could I. If he didn't need a healing miracle to get rid of his scars, then neither did I. Just like him, brokenness didn't have to handicap my living.

Pain, however, did. It clouded my emotions and mind. And it can stop any of us from seeing God's bigger picture. It can hinder us from understanding how all is not lost. God doesn't just pat us on the arm and say, 'No worries. It wasn't that bad.' He does what any of us would do if we noticed a person about to step on to a road with a car headed their way. We would shout, 'Stop! Stop!' We would run and wave our arms. We would repeat ourselves until we caught their attention.

And God feels the same urgency in calling out to us within our pain. He wants to grab our attention and will repeat himself until we get it. Each of us can understand his heart because we too have agonised when our loved ones have suffered from metaphorical meteor strikes.

I could compare it to when Derek and I helped run a summer conference in an old Welsh manor house. The laburnum trees within the gigantic gardens had already produced long, brown seedpods and I pointed out one of the trees to my two young boys. 'Don't eat those seedpods,' I told them. 'I know they look like the peas we grow at home, but these ones are poisonous. Stay away from them.'

A week later, on the way home my youngest son complained of not feeling well, and then he threw up. I put it down to car sickness on those winding Welsh roads. But when he turned white, I asked, 'You don't look so well. Do you hurt somewhere?'

My other son piped up: 'Just before we got into the car, I saw him by the other laburnum tree, the one you didn't say we couldn't eat. I think he ate some.'

Derek and I gasped. People had died from this. 'We need to find a hospital!' I cried, and I pulled out a map. Derek sped down the road. 'Hurry, Derek! Please hurry!' I begged.

'I am! I am!' Derek responded. He pulled up to the front door of a hospital. I jumped out and picked up my now limp son. I dashed through the open front doors. 'My son just ate laburnum seeds,' I cried.

The receptionist pointed back out the front door. 'Go back out, turn left and knock on the brown door.'

I looked at her, horrified. Didn't she care? How could she send me away? I repeated myself. 'My son just ate laburnum seeds! They're poisonous!' I lifted him up higher to show her his limp body just in case she hadn't noticed.

She nodded and pointed again. 'Go back out, turn left and knock on the brown door.'

I hurried out and turned right. 'Turn left! Turn left!' she called.

I found a normal-sized door with no handle on the outside. I stared at it, perplexed. I couldn't even get in. So, I did as instructed and knocked. It opened instantly. 'Come in! Come in!' said a man in a white coat, as if he had been expecting us.

I laid my son on an examining table, and the doctor asked, 'How did you know to come to this hospital? We specialise in poison victims.'

'I didn't,' I replied, and suddenly I understood how God had guided us. More so when the doctor told us we had almost lost our son. We had arrived just in time.

My little son didn't have the ability or capability to save himself, but Derek and I did, the medical staff did. If you noticed, all of us repeated ourselves. All of us used double imperatives: 'Hurry! Hurry!', 'Turn left! Turn left!', 'Come in! Come in!' We had an urgency that demanded attention right now. We had a life-and-death situation, and we rallied around him. We didn't put it off.

God too has this same urgency for our lives. He loves us, just as I loved my little son. He calls out to us urgent words in our pain. He keeps calling out, just as he did to Jerusalem, to the one he had chosen to be his own,[2] the one he called perfect in beauty (Ezekiel 16:14). He loved her.

But despite God's heart for her, Jerusalem had withdrawn from him. She had moved outside his protective love and an enemy army had destroyed her. They had exiled and murdered her people. She was broken. Her past had finally caught up with her. But God refused to let her suffer on her own. He called out to her, with not just one double imperative, but seven in total. His Jerusalem was in pain and perishing.

'Comfort, comfort, my people,' he cried out first of all. 'Speak tenderly to Jerusalem' (Isaiah 40:1–2). He knew that his beloved Jerusalem needed emergency attention, and he was ready to step in. He knew that she couldn't find healing in her heart without his tangible tenderness towards her.

Thankfully, he didn't add, 'Pull yourself together' or 'Get over it.' He simply threw his arms around her, without judgement, without accusation. He knew she had already suffered enough from the consequences of her plans and actions.

Twice in the book of Isaiah God gave Jerusalem the same promise. In her brokenness, he gave her this assurance: 'Those the Lord has rescued will return. They will enter Zion with singing; everlasting joy will crown their heads. Gladness and joy will overtake them, and sorrow and sighing will flee away' (Isaiah 35:10; 51:11). His rescue of her would be so glorious and real that it would become like a precious crown on her head. Just as this crown was his seal of love, so God gives us the same seal as he rescues us. His crown demonstrates his greatest comfort to our hearts – our worth.

Yet we might be thinking, 'This is nice, but I don't want to wear a crown. I just want God to get rid of my troubles. I want him to free me from all that pain, then my worth, comfort and joy would be there anyway.' But God understands our hearts, for even if those troubles were suddenly removed, our hearts don't instantly repair.

Imagine this Bible scene from 2,000 years ago: Paul, a missionary, was at sea (Acts 27). A storm had been raging for days and the ship was in peril of breaking up. But those sailors had the experience to know what to do. They frapped the ship, that is, 'they passed ropes under the ship itself to hold it together' (v. 17). They knew the life-and-death importance of that ship staying in one piece, and God knows the importance of holding us together with his comfort. It enables us to take the next step towards healing our hearts.

Frapping comes in many forms. For the ship, it came from heavy ropes. For Paul, it came from God. An angel appeared to him on that ship, saying, 'Do not be afraid' (v. 24). For us, it could be a hug from a friend, a Bible verse, a smile.

God's encircling comfort is very real. I asked a friend how she had experienced it, and she told me this extreme and unexpected story. Yet it is a story we can all relate to, maybe not in the same level of threat, but all of us have felt unsafe somewhere in our lives.

In my job I trained and supported overseas aid teams. I happened to be in one country during an election and the region where I stayed voted for the losing party. So government soldiers decided to punish the region. They did terrible things.

The aid teams carried urgent medical supplies to the suffering outlying villages, but the government soldiers arrested some of them. And when I and the others heard of this, we immediately hurried to the officials. We told them they should have arrested us instead because we had sent out those teams. I knew we had to do it, but I was filled with dread because of what they could do to us women.

Afterward, we hurried back to our compound, but even there we weren't safe. Only a chain link fence separated us from the soldiers. And when we heard they planned to kill the only male aid worker staying with us, we helped him slip away in the dead of night. How we prayed he would make it to the border safe.

But now, with only women left, we noticed soldier footprints inside the compound. They even rattled at our locked doors. We knew we would be next.

We hid in my bedroom and dressed in layers of clothes, to make it more difficult if we were attacked. We even tucked our documents inside our underwear. Then I telephoned the head office in the capital. I cried as I spoke. 'Please ask my parents to pray. Tell them I probably won't be coming home.'

We crawled under the mosquito net hanging over my bed and clung to each other in fear. We read Psalm 91:

'Surely he will save you from the fowler's snare... You will not fear the terror of night, nor the arrow that flies by day... No harm will overtake you, no disaster will come near your tent.'

Suddenly, we felt calm! We started singing praise songs to God. We laughed. We weren't alone.

The soldiers usually made their attacks between 3.00 am and 4.00 am, the darkest part of the night, but my father had emailed saying he and my mother were praying. He reminded me of 2 Kings 6:13–17, where Elisha and his servant had also been surrounded by enemy soldiers, but God's angel army protected them.

I started praying that this would be true. 'You know,' I said, 'angels are out there protecting us.' And they did. We waited all night and nothing happened, even though dogs barked at the soldiers just outside our fence.

Early the next morning we asked the villagers, 'Why didn't the soldiers attack?' They shook their heads. 'We saw them surround the compound, ready to storm in, but then they left!'

That day a peace-keeping helicopter escorted us out. The man who had to escape in the dead of night got to safety. The imprisoned aid workers were released.

My friend finished her story and we sat in silence. God had comforted her with verses from the Bible and the prayers of those who loved her. She had a hope that defied all logic, and comfort became a precious jewel in her crown, an encircling that held her together. The Bible says, 'Praise be to the God and Father of our Lord Jesus Christ, the Father of compassion and the God of all comfort, who comforts us in all our troubles' (2 Corinthians 1:3–4). God showed my friend her incredible worth.

Comfort is like that. It is a powerful and active word. It is a tender word. The original Hebrew word meant 'to sigh, breathe strongly, to be sorry, to pity, console, to avenge'.[3] It was a word with strong emotions, speaking directly to the heart. It showed the absolute worth of a person, no matter how broken or wounded, no matter their past or hurts.

A young man had just graduated from university and as he looked for a job, he stayed short-term with a family. They noticed his sadness and prayed for him often, that somehow he would experience God's love.

Then one evening their young son fell down the stairs. The mother came running and checked her son. Then she sat down beside him on the floor and hugged him, rocking back and forth. The guest also heard the thumps, and he hurried over. But he remained silent, not saying a word. He just stood there watching.

The mother looked up and assured him that her son was alright, but the visitor didn't seem to hear. Instead, he fixed his eyes, not on the hurting son, but on the mother-son embrace before him. 'When I was a child,' he finally whispered, 'my parents never hugged me. I didn't know it was possible for a parent to love their child like that.'

God saw this young man's deepest hurt and showed him what he needed to see. God reaches out his arms to us, saying, 'As a mother comforts her child, so will I comfort you' (Isaiah 66:13). When we get knocked over by troubles and grief, the first thing he does is comfort us.

A time to reflect

Take a few moments to think about Isaiah 40:1–2: 'Comfort, comfort my people, says your God. Speak tenderly to Jerusalem, and proclaim to her that her hard service has been completed, that her sin has been paid for, that she has received from the Lord's hand double for all her sins.' Consider the following questions:

- What is happening in your life right now? What storms are raging?
- What does the word 'comfort' mean to you now?
- How is God holding your heart together today?
- How can you come to accept your precious worth?

Throughout your day, reflect some more on Isaiah 40:1–2. Write down your thoughts in your journal.

God's comfort: is there hope?

Comfort, comfort my people, says your God. Speak tenderly to Jerusalem.

God's desire to comfort us is ever so real. He calls out to us in our lowest ebbs, for he knows and understands our hearts. He sees our grief, no matter the reasons we are hurting. Yet God's comfort is so much more than simply handing us a tissue and patting us on the back.

It could be compared to an experience I had when I reached my late 20s, with my peace-at-all-costs plan still ruling my life. I had hoped that in time I would get used to my plan, that if I silenced my heart long enough, it would finally stay silenced. But it didn't work. I still had this continuous throbbing knot in my chest, begging me to shout out against the injustices I experienced. But I refused to listen to my inner pain. I didn't dare, for if I did, either grief would overwhelm me or I would have to do something about it.

Then someone sent me a birthday card. This person had never done so before. I tore the envelope open and out fell a ten-dollar bill. I read the message written in the card: 'Dear Eva, it's time you started standing up for your rights. This is for piercing your ears. But, if you don't, I want my money back!'

I almost burst out laughing. The audacity! But this person had judged correctly. I should have fought this battle years before, but as I counted the emotional cost, I doubted I could do it. If I stood up against those long-entrenched injustices, I knew that whatever little bit of me still remained would get shredded. Was it worth it? Was I worth it?

Also, as for piercing my ears, I had been told that real Christians didn't do it, even though no one could substantiate why. So, as I turned the ten-dollar bill over in my hand, I whispered a prayer, 'God, what should I do? I have wanted to get my ears pierced for ages.'

Nothing came to mind, so I slid the bill inside my Bible. I used it as a bookmarker and underlined verses with it. Then I came upon a verse about how God had dressed Jerusalem. To my utter surprise, it said, 'I will put a ring on your nose, earrings on your ears and a beautiful crown on your head… You became very beautiful' (Ezekiel 16:12–13).

It gave me such comfort. All this stifling of myself didn't fit in with God's character. All this severity didn't come from his heart or his love. In fact, God wanted me to pay attention to that pulsating knot in my chest. Since I knew I couldn't change the system around me, I would need to do the changing myself.

About three months later, as I drove home from work, I was overwhelmed by a sudden understanding of my worth in God. I could go with him and break free from the ache I carried in my chest. 'I'll do it!' I whispered. Maybe the ten dollars would be enough to pay for piercing my ears, because I had no money of my own. All my wages went towards paying the family bills.

I detoured to an earring boutique. 'How much does it cost?' I asked, my voice wobbling with uncertainty.

'Ten dollars, my dear,' the lady said. I sighed and laughed, all at once. God had just sorted out the final confirmation, and I handed the lady that ten-dollar bill.

But, as I walked out of that boutique, my earlobes throbbing with pain, I began to shake. What had I just done? What of the repercussions? But God comforted me as I drove away with something I hadn't felt in a very long time – hope. I would be okay. My life belonged to me. I could choose to give it to whom I wanted, and I chose God.

God wants us to listen to our hearts, but he also wants to take us one step further. He desires for his comfort to produce hope in us. 'Comfort, comfort my people, says your God. Speak tenderly to Jerusalem, and proclaim to her that her hard service has been completed' (Isaiah 40:1–2). He promised this to his beloved Jerusalem, and he promises it to us. The hard times will end, whether they are self-inflicted or other-inflicted. He promises a future.

A few years ago, I conducted a survey of women at various stages in life and with different beliefs. I wanted to know which felt more important to them – faith, hope or love. I figured every single woman would say, 'Of course, it is love.'

The answers astonished me. They all said, 'Hope.'

'Why?' I asked one woman.

She explained it well. 'Faith comes and goes, and I have learned to live without love. But hope – if I didn't have hope, I would die. There would be no reason to live.'

How I identified. If hope didn't exist, I would have crumbled in impossible situations. If hope meant nothing, comfort could not have comforted me. Romans 15:13 says, 'May the God of hope fill you with all joy and peace as you trust in him, so that you may overflow with hope by the power of the Holy Spirit.' For us to find comfort, God gives us hope.

So what is hope? Psychologists say that it isn't an emotion.[4] We can learn it and can be taught it. They also say hope is situation specific. We don't need to hope when we feel safe, only when things spiral out of control. We don't need hope when our desires are fulfilled, only when they are outside our grasp. The Bible puts it so well. 'Hope that is seen is no hope at all. Who hopes for what they already have? But if we hope for what we do not yet have, we wait for it patiently' (Romans 8:24–25). Hope is specific to what we don't have.

Yet hope is much more. It is easy to put our hope in people or things that eventually let us down, and through hard experience we find out if we have misplaced our hope. But hope in God is based on fact, that 'the Lord is good, a refuge in times of trouble. He cares for those who trust in him' (Nahum 1:7). It is based on relationship, for 'the Lord delights in those who fear him, who put their hope in his unfailing love' (Psalm 147:11). He wants us to trust in him.

And God never fails. For 'faith is confidence in what we hope for and assurance about what we do not see' (Hebrews 11:1). We can be certain God has our best interests at heart. We can be certain he will give us what is best. He will save us as is best, not necessarily from difficult circumstances, but from the lies that destroy us within those situations. He shows us another way to live.

There is a problem, though. Our mistakes and troubles might have become part of our identity. Several years ago, my family and I stayed in a Welsh mining village in Snowdonia National Park. We wanted to take a break over the Easter holiday and planned to climb a mountain or two.

Very early one morning, while everyone still slept, I went out alone for a prayer walk, down a quiet road that wound around a lake. I sat on a bench overlooking it and I raised my gaze toward Snowdon, the highest peak in Wales. A translucent mist obscured its middle slopes. When the sun finally rose from behind, it shimmered like a wedding veil. I gazed at it, hardly able to breathe.

Then I listened. The silence around me was almost complete, with only the rustle of grass from the marshes behind me. I turned to look, and my eyes rested on the marshes, then on the huge black hills of mining waste behind them. I burst into sobs, weeping not just for the land, but for myself as well.

I had just finished recording my story, about escaping harsh treatment, homelessness and isolation, and those waste heaps visualised my life. The damage done to both of us would remain there forever. Those savage, ugly scars were a permanent part of our landscape, and for me, no amount of comfort or kind words could ever take them away. They couldn't be buried; they would remain with me till my dying breath.

Unexpected emotions surged up inside me. Hopelessness. Horror. How could I live on with such devastation within me? How could I move on with that weight attached to me?

I wanted to scream and pierce the perfect silence. But then I heard a sharp, 'Caw! Caw!'

Turning, I looked again at the waste heaps. A seagull had just spread its wings in flight and the morning sun caught it. It shone bright white against the black. The beauty of light upon dark, of life above carnage, startled me.

I couldn't take my eyes off that seagull as it rose above the devastation and headed towards Mount Snowdon, flapping its wings with lazy ease. It was as if God spoke to me through that bird as it called: 'Caw! I never intended for your past to happen. But the past doesn't have to hold you back. Caw! Fly into all the rest of your life. Follow me into the mountains and all its beauty. Caw! You see, scars don't define you. I do.'

I looked around me with new eyes. The waste hills only took up one-fifth of the landscape. The rest remained untouched and free. My broken past, my thwarted longings, my failings – they took up only a part of my life. The rest remained new and unwritten, a place where I could find meaning and beauty. God had just opened another doorway for me, a doorway into hope, into a mystery yet to be unveiled!

I stretched out my arms in thanks, my wounded heart deeply comforted. I lived! Now I could choose what I did with it! If I wanted, I could stay buried in those barren waste hills, or I could fly away with God, like two seagulls on the wind. Without a moment's hesitation, I accepted God's invitation.

Oh, how often we cry out like Jerusalem, 'The Lord has forsaken me, the Lord has forgotten me' (Isaiah 49:14). But God responds, 'See, I have engraved you on the palms of my hands; your walls are ever before me... Then you will know that I am the Lord; those who hope in me will not be disappointed' (Isaiah 49:16, 23). Hope comes from believing God. Hope comes from knowing that as we stay close to him, he will never leave us. God's comfort is that way. He shows us the truth that he is in charge, and then he helps us to move on emotionally. He enables us to find hope even if our circumstances remain the same.

One young woman shared her story of how God has comforted her, even though her situation hasn't changed.

I wasn't well as a child and spent a lot of time in and out of hospital. Yet no one could figure out what was wrong. I kept passing out, my limbs would go stiff and I felt constantly so exhausted I could barely move. Finally, the doctors decided the attacks were simply growing pains. Then, at age ten, the symptoms stopped.

But when I turned 16, I caught the flu. I never recovered. The attacks started again, but finally the doctors figured it out. They told me there was no cure. I would never get better.

I felt completely lost, as if facing an uphill battle. I had exams to take, I had unexpected problems at home and the stress exacerbated my symptoms. It didn't help that I had no faith back then, no hope. I already felt depressed, and it got a lot worse. I couldn't drag myself out of it.

I began going to a youth group at the local church and one of the leaders sat down with me. 'Where is God in all of this?' I cried out.

The leader didn't get upset. She told me how God uses our difficulties and struggles to build us up into better people, to become more compassionate. But I thought what she said was a load of rubbish. 'Couldn't there be another way?' I asked.

That lady read some verses to me: 'Not only so, but we also glory in our sufferings, because we know that suffering produces perseverance; perseverance, character; and character, hope. And hope does not put us to shame, because God's love has been poured out into our hearts through the Holy Spirit, who has been given to us' (Romans 5:3–5).

And even though I didn't believe her, I kept going back to these verses.

Now, God is a big part of my life, and I want to follow him. But having a chronic pain condition breaks a person down. It makes me exhausted emotionally and physically, and I get into some really low states of mind. I feel so useless. Yet God sees me totally differently.

I am his daughter, and it is something I can't quite comprehend. In my head, I am always striving to be a better person. I never feel good enough, especially when I compare myself to those around. But if I look just at God, I feel there is a purpose for me. In God's sight, I feel pretty perfect. Yes, I am full of sin, but to God I am perfect. This is something I can't register in my head. It is a strange feeling, that unquestionable love of God towards me, and it fills me up when I feel so empty.

This young woman's reality hurt, but she dared to accept God's comfort. She dared to look to God and see his perspective, his bigger picture. She dared to believe him, even in her constant physical pain. She could choose to step into his loving arms. This can be true for us as well.

In our troubles we can hear God say, 'I will lead her into the wilderness and speak tenderly to her. There I will give her back her vineyards, and will make the Valley of [Trouble] a door of hope' (Hosea 2:14–15). In the Bible, God took the hand of his beloved people, and he takes ours. Just as he held them close, he keeps us close. Sure, our troubles might remain, pain might continue, but God has our hearts. We can walk with him through that doorway of hope. A hope and a reminder that, 'Those the Lord has rescued will return. They will enter Zion with singing; everlasting joy will crown their heads. Gladness and joy will overtake them, and sorrow and sighing will flee away' (Isaiah 35:10; 51:11). His crown of comfort – that beautiful symbol of hope.

A time to reflect

Once again, read Hosea 2:14–15: 'I will lead her into the wilderness and speak tenderly to her. There I will give her back her vineyards, and will make the Valley of [Trouble] a door of hope.' Take a moment to reflect on the following questions:

- Of all places, why does God choose to place this door of hope in your valleys?
- What about God gives you hope?
- How can you personally walk through this door of hope?

As you are able, throughout this day, continue to think on Hosea 2:14–15. Record your thoughts in your journal.

2

GOD'S SECOND CALL:
AWAKE! RISE UP!

Awake, awake! Rise up, Jerusalem, you who have drunk from the hand of the Lord.
Isaiah 51:17

God wants Jerusalem to wake up, to see what is going on in her life. And the same is true for us. For in order to heal, we must understand why we hurt.

2

Waking up:
what holds me back?

Awake, awake! Rise up, Jerusalem, you who have drunk from the hand of the Lord.

There was a person who seemed to instinctively know when I was alone at home. Out of the blue, they telephoned, mocking me. They told me that my life was a lie, that I had no rights of my own. I literally trembled as this person spoke… But you might be wondering why I didn't have the courage to hang up, why I didn't defend myself, and why I ever let this person into my life.

At that moment, I yet again slipped back into that keep-the-peace-at-all-costs lie. I yet again forgot how precious I am, how valued and loved by God. I forgot that I could set healthy boundaries. So, when I finally did hang up the phone, I sat and wept; my heart shredded yet again.

The result? My head swirled in confusion. I felt disoriented and couldn't even think of where to turn for help. Then it finally occurred to me that I could ask God. I could involve him in this painful situation. So I prayed that as I escaped the telephone and went out to walk the streets, someone would stop me and specifically ask, 'How are you?'

I had barely stepped out the front door when a relative stranger stopped me. 'How are you?' she asked.

I didn't want to tell her because I didn't really know her. But then I remembered my prayer. God had just answered it, so I took a deep breath and told her what had just happened, but my words came out jumbled. Would she even understand? Would she reject me? I raised a shaky hand to brush away a strand of hair.

'I have been there many times,' she finally said. 'My mother treats me the same way.' Then she told me her story and how she had learned to cope.

As I have thought back on that incident, I noted how my body and mind reacted. Confusion. Stumbling. Poor coordination. Shakiness. I had seen it in others as well, but instead theirs came from drinking too much alcohol. The extreme emotional stress on my body had caused a similar reaction.

At first, I thought I might be overreacting, but later I read how Jerusalem had experienced the same. Her grief was intense, overwhelming, and God understood. He called out to her, 'Therefore, hear this, you afflicted one, made drunk, but not with wine. This is what your Sovereign Lord says, your God, who defends his people: "See, I have taken out of your hand the cup that made you stagger"' (Isaiah 51:21–22). Jerusalem looked like she had been drinking too much wine, but God knew her reactions came from experiencing terrible things – 'ruin and destruction, famine and sword' (Isaiah 51:19). Her children had fainted and lay at every street corner (Isaiah 51:20).

Jerusalem, however, wasn't the only one in the Bible who experienced these drunken symptoms. There was a woman who desperately wanted a child:

> In her deep anguish Hannah prayed to the Lord, weeping bitterly… As she kept on praying to the Lord, Eli [the priest] observed her mouth. Hannah was praying in her heart, and her lips were moving but her voice was not heard. Eli thought she was drunk and said to her, 'How long are you going to stay drunk? Put away your wine.'
> 1 Samuel 1:10, 12–14

Hannah displayed those same drunken symptoms, even though it was her heart which had broken.

It is a natural reaction. Like someone overcome with alcohol, we can crumble to the ground with stupefying grief. We can lie there emotionally numb, unable to function. But thankfully, God doesn't walk by. He gets down beside us, hugging us, comforting us. And just as he cried out that second double imperative to Jerusalem, he cries it out to us as well: 'Awake, awake! Rise up, O Jerusalem, you who have drunk from the hand of the Lord' (Isaiah 51:17). Just as he cradled Jerusalem, he cradles us as we lie there. He calls out for us to open our eyes. He wants us to know that he is right there with us, comforting us, helping us.

You, however, might be wondering what other things cause us to emotionally shut down. You might be wondering if you are there. And if so, how in the world you could get back up again.

In my mid-teens, I attended a summer camp, and how I wanted to become a part of the in-crowd! I watched the camp director interact with other camp counsellors only slightly older than me. They had such fun teasing each other, and I laughed as a spectator at a theatre. But soon I wanted more, to be a part of their fun as well.

I came up with a plan. One day while the director led a meeting, I tiptoed into his cabin and grabbed a pair of his underpants. The next morning before dawn, I hurried to the flagpole. I smiled as I ran it up to the top. That director would slap his knees with laughter and take note of me.

Before breakfast, the whole camp gathered in a large circle around the flagpole. The boy chosen to pull up the camp flag noticed the pants. He solemnly pulled them down, folded them and walked over to the director. 'I believe these belong to you, sir,' he said. I giggled. I couldn't have done it any better.

A ripple of laughter ran around the circle, and the director looked around at the counsellors, his eyes twitching with mirth. 'Who did this?' he asked, a lilt in his voice.

I raised my hand, smiling. 'Me!'

His eyes suddenly grew hard. He said nothing. But afterward, as the field emptied for breakfast, he signalled for me to come over. 'You insulted me in front of everyone,' he said. 'You will go to every single person in this camp, and you will apologise. And don't you ever do anything like this again.'

How I grieved. I had judged it so wrong. That director had no interest in including me. Instead, I had offended him and now I would hurt myself as well, the consequences lasting for decades. As I stumbled from person to person in that camp, I vowed never to be funny again, never to be myself. For me, the cost felt just too high. I figured it was easier to be a quiet little mouse of a person than to fight for who I was. It was easier to shut my personality down, and I went to sleep emotionally.

Fourteen years passed. I became a counsellor at that very same camp, this time with another director. At the awards evening the MC called my name. 'We would like to present Eva with a special honour. Everyone in camp agrees with this – Eva, the gentlest person ever!'

I hurried forward to the applause, smiling. It felt so nice to get noticed, to know everyone liked me. Then a light switched on inside me, as if I was waking up. Yes, I might be the gentlest person around – never contradicting, always helping, always smiling, no matter how I felt – but that wasn't who I really was. I had conformed to a past director's anger, and this had become my identity. These people didn't know me, and even I had forgotten. I felt like a fraud.

Instead of rectifying it, I went to sleep again and stayed that way, because I still felt too scared to explore my heart. For if this camp director didn't like me, maybe there was nothing to like, maybe I had no worth. His opinion of me chained me down like a prisoner. That is, until Derek began to understand this a couple of years into our marriage.

'Eva,' he said, 'what I am going to say will probably make married life uncomfortable for me. It has been easy for me up to this point. You always serve me and never contradict me. But I'm beginning to realise this isn't right. This isn't what a relationship should be like. I am going to start asking your opinion on everything, and please don't tell me what you think I want to hear. I want to hear what *you* think. I want to know what *you* want.'

Now, you might think this sounded like heaven to my ears, to finally feel the freedom to be myself, to finally be able to say what I thought. Instead, it tore me apart. What if Derek reprimanded me for taking an initiative? What if he too turned hostile towards me? What if I entrusted to him who I really was, and he rejected me?

I am so thankful Derek took the risk, that he called me to wake up. Even though I felt tempted to stay asleep, something deep in my heart yearned to be true to myself. If God loved me unconditionally, if he had made me, I could trust him that the true me would be okay in this world. It would take courage, but with him, I would be okay. I didn't have to live in fear of myself or others anymore.

The people of Israel experienced this as well. They had escaped from slavery, but fear still ruled their lives. Now, as their enemies surrounded them on all sides, this fear raised its ugly head. They could see the powerful enemy and nothing else. But their leader opened their eyes. He said, 'Be strong and courageous. Do not be afraid or terrified because of them, for the Lord your God goes with you; he will never leave you nor forsake you' (Deuteronomy 31:6). If they could only wake up in their minds and see the whole picture, they would know God had things in hand.

The apostle Paul wrote something similar: 'Everything exposed by the light becomes visible – and everything that is illuminated becomes a light. This is why it is said, "Wake up, sleeper, rise from the dead, and Christ will shine on you"' (Ephesians 5:13–14). Paul called out to a fledgling church and asked them to have the courage to wake up. When they did, their perspective would change. They would see Jesus at work.

However, we might still be too scared to choose to wake up, especially if we are responsible for the chaos in our lives, or there are situations out of our control. We might think that understanding the situation will cause us even more pain and decide it is safer to go back to sleep. We bury the pain and pretend it never happened.

God doesn't want us to fear waking up. Yes, it may be painful, but he is with us. For as we respond to God's second call, 'Awake, awake,' he shows us what he is able to do: 'Strengthen the feeble hands, steady the knees that give way; say to those with fearful hearts, "Be strong, do not fear; your God will come, he will come with vengeance; with divine retribution he will come to save you"' (Isaiah 35:3–4). God wants us to know that he himself is with us in our anxieties, our hurts and our griefs. He keeps encouraging us not to back down.

It is like when a neighbour came to my house one afternoon, with eyes swollen and hardly able to breathe. She held a pot of lilies as far away from her as possible. 'Would you like this?' she said, handing me the pot. 'Someone just gave it to me as a present, but I'm allergic to lilies. The doctor says I have a choice, it is me or them.'

I took them, but then I stopped. 'I'm sorry. I can't. We have a cat. Lilies are fatal to cats. I know of a couple that died. Their owners didn't know lilies were poisonous, and they had a bouquet in their house. Maybe there is someone else who would like them.'

My neighbour looked horrified, and then she laughed. 'I'm so sorry, but I don't want to throw these lilies away. Do you know of someone who might like them? I don't care who. A neighbour. Someone at church.'

At that moment, another neighbour appeared. Our eyes lit up and we nodded to each other. We headed her way, explaining our problem, and this new neighbour laughed. 'Oh, yes, please! I love lilies.'

Each of us women were awake. We understood our limitations and we lived within them. We also found the courage to say so to each other.

But what if my neighbour had kept those lilies because she didn't have the emotional strength to say 'no'? What if she didn't want to offend the giver? She would have felt miserable. She would have probably blamed the person who had given her those flowers and grumbled at their insensitivity. She would have probably blamed God for allowing those lilies to come into her house, even feeling betrayed by him. She would have called out to God, 'Wake up! Don't you know that I'm allergic to lilies?'

Jerusalem said the exact same thing. Life had become too much of a misery and she shouted out a bold double imperative to God himself: 'Awake, awake, arm of the Lord, clothe yourself with strength! Awake, as in days gone by' (Isaiah 51:9). As far as Jerusalem understood, God should take the responsibility for all the bad that had happened to her. He should wake up, get to work and use his superpowers. Wasn't he supposed to protect her from the consequences of her actions? Wasn't he supposed to make her wrong choices go away? He was shirking in his responsibility to keep her safe.

Thankfully, God didn't stomp off in an injured huff. Instead, he used her own words and spoke them back: 'Awake, awake! Rise up, Jerusalem… you afflicted one, made drunk, but not with wine' (Isaiah 51:17, 21). It was a masterful twist. God showed her that she had deflected her problems on to him. For any of us, this is a scary place to be, to see that maybe when things go wrong, we might be contributors.

A young girl had been diagnosed with learning disabilities, but her mother thought she was coping alright. Every spare moment this little girl had she spent drawing pictures in her colouring pad. Yet one day, as her mother walked by, this child hid her pad.

She hid it again the next day, and the next. 'Is everything okay?' her mother finally asked. The young girl nodded.

Every day after that, the daughter hid her pictures. The mother realised that something must be wrong, and she filled with fear. But she didn't want to project this unease on to her child, especially if she had imagined it.

A week later the mother couldn't bear the barrier between her and her little daughter any longer. She stopped and asked if her daughter wouldn't mind showing her just one picture. The young girl hesitated and then opened her pad, keeping it close to her chest.

She flicked through it and then stopped. She lowered it on to her lap, showing a bouquet of bright yellow sunflowers. 'How lovely,' her mother said, relieved. Then she bent down close and took a better look.

Each brown centre of each golden sunflower had a little face drawn inside. Each one had small translucent tears running down their cheeks. Tears ran down her daughter's face as well.

The mother's heart quaked yet again. Had someone hurt her daughter without her knowing? 'Why are you sad?' she whispered, dreading what might be the answer.

The young girl opened her heart and talked about school. Children teased her for not being able to tell time, for not being able to spell or read. They called her stupid. But the daughter hadn't wanted to tell her mother, even though it had been going on for over a month. Her mother always looked so busy, and this child hadn't wanted to bother her.

Her mother finally woke up and understood the problem. She comforted her daughter, and the next day they both went to school. She stood up for her daughter. She accepted her responsibility to re-establish caring boundaries for her daughter, and she stepped out with courage and strength. But she also had to address another problem, that of personally being too busy. She began to work on it in practical ways.

As we grow aware of the root causes of our troubles, it might mean that we should change something in our lives. Or we could simply respond by ignoring it or shut down in fear. But Jesus calls out to us, 'Take courage! It is I. Don't be afraid' (Matthew 14:27). Just as he encouraged his disciples to not hide in fear, he wants us to be courageous and look each situation in the face. With his comforting arms around us, we can.

A time to reflect

Reread Isaiah 51:17 several times. Waking up is one of the most courageous things we can do. 'Awake, awake! Rise up, Jerusalem, you who have drunk from the hand of the Lord the cup of his wrath, you who have drained to its dregs the goblet that makes people stagger.' Consider the following questions:

- What is making your heart stagger in life?
- Why do you think it is affecting you so much?
- What about God would help you live with courage?

As you have time, continue reflecting on Isaiah 51:17. Record your thoughts in your journal.

Waking up:
where is God?

Awake, awake! Rise up, Jerusalem, you who have drunk from the hand of the Lord.

There is a risk when waking up. God knows that as we do, we may begin to doubt him. We may begin to question our relationship with him, even though he is comforting us in our hard times, even though we know he has our best interests at heart.

As I grew up, I often listened to heated discussions on theology around the kitchen table, and there were always two sides: those who believed in God and those who didn't. Opposite me sat a beloved relative, and after one such discussion I slipped my hand in hers. 'Are you a Christian?' I asked. She shook her head. I was only ten, and that evening I wept into my pillow. How could someone not love God? How could anyone not believe?

The foundations of my life shifted that night. I suddenly understood a terrible fact: not everyone cared about God, not everyone believed in him, even though being a Christian seemed so obvious to me. Yet decades later, I too considered stepping over to the other side. What had been unthinkable to me as a girl suddenly became a viable option. It didn't matter that I had been a Christian for over 30 years or that I had a degree from a Bible college. It began when Derek, our little children and I moved to another country as missionaries.

Not long after we arrived, a local woman approached me and looked me straight in the eye. 'Madam, I can see you love your daughter. You must never let her out of your sight. I assure you; she will get kidnapped. It happens. With her blonde hair and blue eyes, she will disappear.'

I believed this woman and my maternal instincts kicked into overdrive. I looked after my daughter like a hovering hawk. In public, I never let her out of my sight. But I had to give her freedom as well, and when we went into town and sat in the plaza, I let her run free around the fountain. A couple of times strange men in business suits grasped her by the hand and started to lead her away. I ran after them, shouting, grabbing my daughter back.

Also, in the block of flats where we rented, prostitutes decided to set up business. They worked in the apartment next to ours and late at night I could hear them through the walls. Not only that, but our balconies sat side by side, and one day a stranger began chatting with my daughter. He reached over and stroked her hair. Anger surged up within me.

I ran outside and grabbed her away. I couldn't get her inside fast enough. My five-year-old daughter wasn't even safe in her own home.

My list of grievances grew the longer we lived overseas: loneliness such as I had never experienced; human excrement smeared on the wall by our front door; witchcraft, trying to destroy our children and our marriage; speeding cars that just missed us by inches – one time the wing mirror brushed my sweater; my sons got beaten up.

I looked up towards heaven, fully aware of what was happening, fully awake, but with resentment in my heart. We had gone out to tell of God's love, but he had allowed our destruction instead. I couldn't understand why. I had given God everything, trusted him, sacrificed for him, yet he refused to protect us. Didn't he care? Wasn't he aware?

As far as I understood, our relationship was over. He had broken trust with me. I had already put up with far too much abuse growing up, and I had learned my lesson. I wouldn't tolerate it anymore. Judgement time had come.

God hung in the balance. I wandered around the house in deathly silence, darkness wrapped around me like a shroud. I felt like a woman contemplating divorce, fingering her wedding ring. Should I turn my back on God? Should I stop being a Christian? But perhaps even these questions were not valid. What if God didn't exist?

If this was true, I had deceived myself. Oh, the agony! I had given my life for nothing. I had risked my children's lives for a delusion. I might as well do what Jerusalem had done when she rejected God and he warned her of the trouble coming her way. She simply laughed and replied, 'Let us eat and drink… for tomorrow we die!' (Isaiah 22:13). I too should enjoy whatever I wanted and go out with a bang.

This, however, centred around me, about what I felt. If God didn't exist, was there anything else worthwhile to believe in, to live for? I didn't know.

I dug deep in my heart. I searched my life for clues. Things had happened that I could never have engineered, like escaping from an abusive house, like having a husband who loved me, like being able to have four children, despite five miscarriages. Yes. There certainly was evidence of something out there. Could it be God?

Yet if he did exist, my opinion of him must be woefully wrong. I had figured in my imagination what he should be like. I wanted a compliant God, soft and comforting, just like a teddy bear. I wanted a spandex superhero with only one aim in mind, to rescue me from the messes I had made and from the meteor strikes headed my way. I wanted a butler in a black suit and bow tie, someone to keep my life ordered and simple. But the actual God I now encountered clashed with my perceptions. His unpredictability scared me. If he wanted, he could slay me. He could ignore me and not do anything I wanted. He was God, uncontrolled by me or the world, because 'our God is in heaven; he does whatever pleases him' (Psalm 115:3).

I didn't know this kind of God. I didn't even like what it meant. But I could see no one else out there to whom I could turn. No one else who could set me free. No one who could fill his shoes. No one.

For two days the foundations in my life shook with seismic violence. But within that time a verse kept coming to mind. 'Without faith it is impossible to please God, because anyone who comes to him must believe that he exists and that he rewards those who earnestly seek him' (Hebrews 11:6). I might have been evaluating whether God was real, or not, but then I woke up in a deeper way. Maybe God was evaluating me, asking me if I was real? Did I have what it takes to live without fear, to take the risk of living in uncertainty? Could I run with God?

I shivered at how close I came to discarding him. But, for better or worse, for richer or poorer, I would choose to remain with God. I would walk with him, not into the comfortable and protected life I demanded from him, that I so craved in my growing-up years, but into a place of yielding to him. I would let go of what I thought was best for me and walk into the rest of my life with his heart for me.

I slipped my metaphorical wedding ring back on and stepped into an unknown that frightened me out of my wits. Who was this God I now chose to follow? I had built my life on faulty ideas of him. I had better get started all over again.

God knows that when we wake up, we may question the very essence of what we believe. He knows that pain and trouble can cause us to doubt his existence, and even doubt and mistrust those around us. He knows that grief can confuse us, and it is hard to find a way out. God, however, doesn't leave us. Just like Jerusalem, we can find our way back to him. Just like Jerusalem, we can cry out to him for help. He said, 'People of Zion, who live in Jerusalem, you will weep no more. How gracious he will be when you cry for help! As soon as he hears, he will answer you' (Isaiah 30:19). Just as God responded to her with kindness and love, he does the same to us. Even though the scenes around us may be overwhelming, as we call out to him, he stands with us. He promises us his way out of every impossible situation.

Doubt, however, is creative in its mindset and it can take us down further trails of thought. As we experience troubles, it can creep in, making us question God's love for us. For doubt will stop us from waking up to what God wants us to see.

It is like the story a friend shared with me. Let's call her Becks.

I sensed so much sadness in the world, things that happened which couldn't be undone, things which people would never have a chance to experience. Even the Bible agreed with me. 'What is crooked cannot be straightened; what is lacking cannot be counted' (Ecclesiastes 1:15).

All I saw was brokenness around me, and I felt I had no right to be hopeful and happy. I could see what was missing and never be fixed. As a Christian, I knew I should be happy, but instead, I wanted to cry.

After a while, I couldn't cope with the tension and asked a pastor and lady to pray for me. They asked me questions and it brought up my past, about how my mother had told me we were identical in every way. And as I shared, I knew deep down inside that this was wrong. I wanted to break free.

Yet I felt so vulnerable, like I consisted of tiny pieces, all held together by a thread. And if I opened up to a big and powerful God, I might just disappear. It terrified me to think that he could crush me.

The pastor asked if I could forgive my mother and myself as well. But I couldn't pray, I felt that scared. Then an image came to the lady's mind. She said, 'I see a little girl who is supposed to be doing the dishes, but instead she runs outside with soap bubbles still on her arms. She looks up into the sky and sees a rainbow.'

That got my attention, because it had been raining all morning, and when the sun broke through, I had searched the sky for a rainbow, that symbol of hope. But there had not been one, so I had no hope. I felt I had nothing left... And now, a few hours later, this lady told me about a little girl that represented me!

My picture of God suddenly changed. I knew that God stood beside me, and even though I still felt worthless, he would never crush me. He would never condemn me. I didn't need a sign of hope. I now knew that God saw me and cared for me, that he would be gentle with me.

I prayed for God to forgive me, for always seeing what was missing. I prayed for help to leave this negativity behind. I prayed that I could choose hope. I prayed that I would learn to forgive my mother and begin to look at life through different eyes. I prayed that I would think positively about myself, and the Lord took my pieces, moulding me into someone free to love.

This heart-searching story shows the utter imperative to understand which voice is God's. He wants us to wake up to his truth, that he is with us, that he deeply cares. Any other opinion is a lie. He says, 'When you pass through the waters, I will be with you; and when you pass through the rivers, they will not sweep over you. When you walk through the fire, you will not be burned; the flames will not set you ablaze' (Isaiah 43:2). He says, 'Do not fear, for I am with you; do not be dismayed, for I am your God. I will strengthen you and help you; I will uphold you with my righteous right hand' (Isaiah 41:10). Truly waking up comes from knowing that what he says is unequivocally true.

Peter, one of Jesus' disciples, experienced this first-hand. He and his friends rowed across a lake, and when they saw Jesus walking on the surface of the water, they cried out in fear, thinking him a ghost. But Peter pulled himself together and called, 'Lord, if it's you… tell me to come to you on the water'.

Jesus stretched out his hand – 'Come!' – because he knew Peter could do it if his focus was right.

Peter climbed on to the water and hurried towards Jesus. But the waves crashed around him and he took his eyes off Jesus. His surroundings distracted his attention. His logic kicked in, questioning his judgement. As he doubted himself and the invitation Jesus gave him, he began to sink. 'Lord, save me!' he cried.

Jesus instantly caught him, but said, 'You of little faith… why did you doubt?'[5]

Doubt in God will do this to us. It is a mindset that makes us sink, because we forget who God is and in essence go to sleep to what is true. We forget that God can see us. We forget that he's right there, ready to catch us. We stumble through life. We lose our courage and strength.

One Sunday morning, I arrived at church and a stranger stood by the refreshment table wearing an ill-fitting suit. It must have been three inches too short on his legs and arms, and it looked to me like he had simply come for the free food and coffee. I hurried past him, my nose in the air, but somehow feeling unsafe as well. I too had lived like him, homeless as a young woman, hungry because we ran out of food, dishevelled because we couldn't afford proper clothes. I never wanted that to happen again. It still hurt too much, even years later.

It did occur to me that I should be polite and talk with this person, but I fled. I took a seat near the front of the church, waiting for the service leader to introduce the guest speaker. You guessed it – it was that man. 'I must apologise for my suit,' he said. 'Yesterday, when I left home, I forgot to bring mine along, so I picked this one up at one of your local charity shops. It was the only one which sort of fit!'

I choked with grief. I had shut myself down and excluded that man because of my past. But I had also pushed God out. I doubted his goodness in letting this man step into my life. I doubted God's kindness in reminding me of terrible times, that he always had my back and got me through. Those wasted years were like treasures in his eyes, places where I learned about strength and perseverance, hope, dignity and the utter value of every person on earth. This included me and that speaker. I sat there in church and remembered.

A week later, as I drove into town, the traffic ground to a halt. A foreign semi-truck sat at a roundabout, just ahead of me. It kept signalling one way and then the other. I could tell the driver was lost.

I waited in my car, drumming my fingers on the steering wheel. Cars pulled out behind me, honking their horns. They zoomed past, shooting angry glares at the driver in the truck. But they gave me no space to escape with them either. I sat there stuck behind that truck.

Feelings began to rise in my heart. As a young woman, I too had been treated as strange, with no home, no normality in life, living in a tent for months. People had laughed at me and rejected me. They had jeered and told me to go away. I could have been the perfect person to help that driver because I understood rejection and feeling lost. But I couldn't see why I should face my past, when all I wanted to do was forget it.

Was God mocking my pain yet again? Did he not care about my heart? But at that moment, I heard a roar. A biker rode up beside the truck, with chrome, black leather and a long ponytail hanging down his back. He stopped beside the truck and raised his tinted visor. They exchanged words, and the biker waved his hand in a 'follow me' kind of way. He pulled out in front of the truck and the truck driver followed him.

I grieved yet again. Could I ever find the strength to break free from doubting God's goodness to me? Would I always keep forgetting that because of him, I could accept the situations and people he brought to me? My past had left me a frightened prisoner, and now God was waking me up. He was declaring to me a terrible fact, that fear had been a controller for most of my life, not him.

God wanted me to acknowledge it and let it go. He would enable me to live with courage. I didn't have to doubt him. I didn't have to think that this was the only way I was doomed to live. I could accept his perspective of what was right and good.

God never gives up on us. Troubles may overwhelm us, but as we wake up, he gives us a tenacity to look life full in the face. As we humbly embrace what God wants us to see, he gives us a second jewel in our crown, because 'the Lord takes delight in his people; he crowns the humble with victory' (Psalm 149:4). Yes, God delights in you and me. He shows the world who we are – his victorious, crown-wearing daughters. This is a fact.

A time to reflect

Spend some time thinking about Isaiah 43:2, 'When you pass through the waters, I will be with you; and when you pass through the rivers, they will not sweep over you. When you walk through the fire, you will not be burned; the flames will not set you ablaze.' Please consider the following questions:

- Is God waking you up to things which hold you back? What are they?
- Which verses about God give you the assurance that you can face them?
- How can his promises help you remain true?

As you have time, think more on Isaiah 43:2. Record your thoughts in your journal.

3

GOD'S THIRD CALL: AWAKE! GET DRESSED!

Awake, awake, Zion, clothe yourself with strength! Put on your garments of splendour.

Isaiah 52:1

A loving call for Jerusalem to wear the clothes God gave her. And a loving call for each one of us to accept his clothes of strength and courage, for then we can move on.

Waking up: how much am I loved?

Awake, awake, Zion, clothe yourself with strength! Put on your garments of splendour.

The next stage of getting up is getting dressed. For after God has comforted us, then called us to wake up and open our eyes, he cries out a third double imperative: 'Awake, awake, Zion, clothe yourself with strength! Put on your garments of splendour, Jerusalem, the holy city' (Isaiah 52:1). Just as God cared about what Jerusalem wore, he also cares about our clothes. What we wear really matters.

It is important, however, to first recognise why we need these new clothes. If you remember, Jerusalem had collapsed with grief, but those who had hurt her rubbed it in. They said, '"Fall prostrate that we may walk on you." And [Jerusalem] made [her] back like the ground, like a street to be walked on' (Isaiah 51:23). Jerusalem didn't wake up to find herself among clean sheets. Instead, she woke up on the street. She was filthy. Her clothes were ruined and whatever dignity she had left had been trampled underfoot by her persecutors. They had trashed her, and she knew it.

But God saw her differently. And God sees us differently. He urgently calls out for us to put on strength when we wake up to the fact that we are feeling helpless and treated badly. He clothes us with splendour where we feel belittled, where others think they have the right to use us. In God's sight these clothes give us identity. They give us God's splendour and the strength to get up and live.

As a child, I grew up in a farming community. One of the farmers had a young wife who always wore jeans, her long blonde hair always pulled back tight in a ponytail. I saw how hard she worked, driving tractors, shovelling muck and feeding over 100 milk cows. Yet one day she came to a wedding at our local church, her hair curled and wearing a short yellow dress. She looked like a super model on the front cover of a glossy magazine! The only thing which linked this beauty to a farmer's wife were her broken and stained nails. Suddenly her identity within the community changed.

The clothes we wear express who we are, and it is the same with the clothes God has for us. There are, however, many more garments in God's wardrobe. Isaiah, the prophet says, 'My soul rejoices in my God. For he has clothed me with garments of salvation and arrayed me in a robe of his righteousness' (Isaiah 61:10). God not only gives us identity, but he also gives us clothes for our heart, so we can go out and live despite what we are going through.

God cares that we have all we need to live well – his garments of salvation for delivering us and keeping us safe, for our well-being; his robe of righteousness for having our backs and standing up for us, for helping us live truthfully and like champions.[6] Yet we might be saying, 'Okay, God, I hear that, but I don't understand what this means practically, especially when I don't feel any change.'

In my work I regularly meet up with women. We chat about life, do a half-hour Bible study and then spend some time praying for each other. At the end of one such meeting, I bowed my head and prayed, 'Dear Jesus, I thank you that you are in control of everything. [I sighed here, a resigned sort of sigh.] I trust you to...'

The woman I was meeting with interrupted me. 'Eva! You're angry with God!'

I looked up, startled. She sat on the sofa, leaning forward, shock in her eyes. I shook my head. How could she have come to this conclusion? 'No, I'm not!' I said.

'Yes, you are!'

Well, our prayer time ended and she left soon afterward, but I remained on the sofa, disturbed. I knew this woman. Even though I was supposed to be helping her, she often spoke to my heart. I knew I had to pay attention to her words, so I prayed, 'God, am I angry with you?'

Nothing came to mind, so I searched my heart. Oh, groan! That woman had understood correctly! I was still furious with God, even though I had left home years before. I had forgiven those who had wounded me as a young woman, but I hadn't forgiven God. Why hadn't he stopped it when I begged him again and again?

I sat in stunned silence. Was it even right to consider forgiving God? After all, he was perfect and never did anything wrong. But whether right or not, I held a deep grudge and, without realising, I had distanced myself from him. I served him, but at arm's length. I followed him, but with caution and reservation. I let the pain in my life take control of my relationship with him.

I didn't know what to do. Would this result in God rejecting me? But then it occurred to me that he had known all along and still he loved me. It wasn't a shock when I finally admitted it. Even though he had been aware of how my pain had affected me for the decades I carried it, he hadn't brought it up until I could hear.

The thought of God loving me to this extent, that he could overlook my painful attitude and still work with me, overwhelmed me. I began to write in my journal:

> Dear God, you never once justified yourself in all those years. Instead, you waited patiently for me to come to you. Please be the Father you have always wanted to be. Please teach me to be the daughter I want to be. I just need to come. Here I am.

Like the prodigal son, I came back to God in a deeper way than I ever could have known. I was his prodigal daughter. I had taken out my anger on him and now I had come home, not because someone forced me, but of my own free will. I acknowledged that my pain had got the better of me, and now I wanted to restore a fractured relationship. Just as that father treated the prodigal with love even though he hadn't earned it, so did God. I received his clothes of salvation and righteousness, of being rescued and accepted as I was.

I personalise the Bible story: 'The father said to his servants, "Quick! Bring the best robe and put it on her. Put a ring on her finger and sandals on her feet… Let's have a feast and celebrate. For this daughter of mine was dead and is alive again; she was lost and is found"' (Luke 15:22–24). But God had another surprise for me as well. Without knowing any of this, someone gave me a gift so I could buy a new dress, something I hadn't done in years. How I laughed. My Father God in heaven had welcomed me home and given me new clothes, not just for my heart, but practically as well.

My friend Alice also understood and embraced God's clothing for herself. One day she told me the following story.

I first felt God's love as a nine- or ten-year-old. I had just come back from a school trip, and for some reason my parents were late in collecting me. I waited outside the school gate with the teacher. It was dark. I don't remember a streetlight, as the school was on the outskirts of town. But my biggest worry was the Yorkshire Ripper who was still at large. I had heard reports of murders in our area. Yet out of the blue I felt held by God's love. I felt great peace, and an incredible sense of God with me. I would be okay.

I experienced God's love at university as well when I felt desperately lonely. I experienced it when I started dating my husband. I experienced it when my husband died. I realised that grief was a gift – God trusting me that I could be on my own and look after two small children. God trusting me even when it felt bleak. He loved me. He strengthened me. And each of these incidents became like a pearl, added on a string, hanging around my neck.

Alice saw God's clothing as a part of her life. She accepted his jewellery, the gifts he chose to give. She would never have wanted her husband to die, but in her grief, she saw God's hand. She gave him permission to work in her life and he pulled out beauty where only sadness reigned. This is what God did for his beloved Jerusalem, to 'provide for those who grieve in Zion – to bestow on them a crown of beauty instead of ashes, the oil of joy instead of mourning, and a garment of praise instead of a spirit of despair' (Isaiah 61:3). God gave my friend his most precious gift – love. His clothes would protect her heart and keep her emotions secure.

God is like that. Yet it may be hard to think of a new wardrobe when we are experiencing grief. This is why God takes us through a process – of comfort, of waking us up to look around, then showing us the garments he provides. When we are hurting, all we can think of is darkness, pain and revulsion. But God sees beyond our circumstances and sees us as beautiful and beloved women, deserving the best as his daughters.

There is other clothing God wants us to wear, especially when we are battling griefs and hurts in our lives, the evil we see around us. The Bible tells us, 'Be alert and of sober mind. Your enemy the devil prowls around like a roaring lion looking for someone to devour. Resist him, standing firm in the faith' (1 Peter 5:8–9). God knows we have an enemy who is out to destroy us and those we love. He knows we need battle gear if we are going to fight well. He gives us an armoury if we accept.

The Bible lists each item:

> Stand firm then, with the belt of truth buckled round your waist, with the breastplate of righteousness in place, and with your feet fitted with the readiness that comes from the gospel of peace. In addition to all this, take up the shield of faith, with which you can extinguish all the flaming arrows of the evil one. Take the helmet of salvation and the sword of the Spirit, which is the word of God.
> EPHESIANS 6:14–17

If you notice, much of this list we have already mentioned. Truth – seeing things the way God sees them. Righteousness – accepting God's opinion of us. Peace – embracing that God is in control. Faith – knowing that God won't let us down. The Bible – our constant source of comfort and guidance.

The way we stand firm will make or break our fight with the ultimate enemy. He is out to destroy our hearts, but we don't have to resist him unprotected and alone. 'For the Lord your God is the one who goes with you to fight for you against your enemies to give you victory' (Deuteronomy 20:4). With God we can regain the victory the devil robbed from us, even though we may have changed and life looks different now.

However, it is good to remember that the devil doesn't wear a sign around his neck advertising his intentions. He doesn't send us a manual of his tactics for destroying lives. Instead, he tries to subversively turn our hearts against God, and he can use our pain to cause us havoc.

This happened to David when he 'learned that Saul had come out to take his life' (1 Samuel 23:15). David fled, a frightened young man. His strength was failing. But he had a friend, Jonathan, who 'went to David… and helped him find strength in God. "Don't be afraid," [Jonathan] said. "My father Saul will not lay a hand on you"' (vv. 16–17). This is what God does. Because he loves us, he knows that there will be times when we grow weak, and his garments begin to slip from our shoulders. So he sends us help to hang in there.

Because of his pain, David could have pushed his friend away, but he accepted the help extended to him. He let his friend come close in his darkest hour, even when he might have experienced shame at feeling weak or doubting that God was enough. And even though his armour was slipping off, he let Jonathan help him keep it on. Through his friend, he could regain God's perspective. For, as each of us knows, when the pain is the fiercest, doubts creep in, causing us to question God's love for us.

Someone once told me that in ancient times, when metal armour was worn in battle, sometimes the enemy catapulted a beehive into the opposition's camp. The bees would go wild, getting under the opposition's armour, and out of agony the soldiers would tear it off. Now they were vulnerable and exposed to arrows. They could get picked off one by one. The same is true for us. Once we put our armour on, the enemy will try to force us out by playing on our doubts and griefs. This almost happened to the young woman who suffered from constant physical pain.

I went to a youth camp run by my youth leader and learned about God. I saw God's love. It was the highlight of my year and a defining time in my life. Then, when I turned 18, my youth leader asked me to join the organising team. I was about to start university as well. But with family problems, where I needed to act like a parent, I had to drop out of university. It came as such a huge blow, and I fell to pieces.

One of the camp leaders sat me down and asked me if something was wrong. I told her, and she, a woman I hardly knew, offered for me to move into her house. She arranged a part-time job for me. She and her family stood with me the whole time, even though I was especially broken when I moved in.

This woman never gave up on me. She said she wanted to give me the space to develop my own identity and not be consumed by what was happening back home. It was amazing, a huge thing for a family to do. They took me on with all my emotional baggage, even though they didn't know me. They gave their time to help heal some of my wounds. In the end, I lived with them for 18 months.

But the good news didn't stop there. Back home, problems got sorted out, and this strengthened my faith as well. So many answers to prayer, ones I never expected. But then, I never do, for every answer always comes as a surprise.

Now, three years on, I still must spend half of my week in bed. I'm still on a lot of painkillers and medicine. I still struggle, but I have God and I have people around me who love me. I still see that woman and her family once a week.

This amazing story would never have happened if that family hadn't stepped in and helped this young woman overcome deep inner pain. They helped her keep God's armour on. Because she accepted the love extended to her, God gave her victory – not the kind where everything turns out nice and easy, but the kind where a warrior leans on her sword, exhausted, wounded, but full of hope.

The Bible says, 'God is love' (1 John 4:16), yet he respects our choices, and he delights when we accept the clothes he gives. It is through his clothes that we discover how beloved we are. It is with his clothes that we can live with splendour and strength, with salvation and righteousness, with armour that keeps us safe. As we choose them, we can say, 'I have fought the good fight, I have finished the race, I have kept the faith. Now there is in store for me the crown of righteousness, which the Lord, the righteous Judge, will award to me on that day' (2 Timothy 4:7–8). We can accept this wonderful part of our apparel – a warrior's crown.

A time to reflect

Take a few moments to reread Isaiah 52:1: 'Awake, awake, Zion, clothe yourself with strength! Put on your garments of splendour, Jerusalem.' Ponder the following questions:

- In what area of life do you feel robbed of worth, dignity or love?
- What part of God's wardrobe or armour do you need especially today?
- Is there a friend you can ask to help you remember God and all he has given you?

Throughout your day, as you are able, think some more about Isaiah 52:1. Record your thoughts in your journal. And if you feel able, get in touch with a friend.

Waking up:
what about my rags?

Awake, awake, Zion, clothe yourself with strength! Put on your garments of splendour.

Three years into marriage and out of the blue, a series of metaphorical meteors struck me thick and fast. It started with the miscarriage of my second child, when a sense of depression enfolded me for months. During this time, a woman I deeply respected took me aside and said:

> Eva, I am so disappointed with you. You say you are a Christian, but you don't show it. You don't even know how to love. Non-Christians love me better than you. Just because you're educated doesn't make you better than me. If you loved me, you would do what I want. I really don't know what to do with you.

I stared at the person, speechless, as she went on. Her sudden vehemence caught me off guard and I simply couldn't move. Only after she had finished could I find the presence of mind to get up without a word and escape. I staggered away and wept behind closed doors. I had entrusted my heart to a person I thought had loved and respected me, but instead I had been torn to shreds.

Several months later I fell pregnant again, and still, I couldn't stop weeping. I worried that my reaction would affect my unborn child. This, however, was only the beginning. In the space of that year, two family members died and another had a horrific car accident. To top it off, at one of the funerals, Derek developed strange walnut-sized lumps on his lower legs. We hurried home for a series of tests and the doctor told us Derek had a condition called sarcoidosis. It would be with him for the rest of his life, though if things went well it could go into remission. But it left Derek breathless and exhausted, flat in bed most days.

I wept again. What was I supposed to do? I had only lived in Britain for three short years, and I still felt a stranger. I had a toddler. I was pregnant. And because we had decided to join a Christian charity and the plans had been laid to move, Derek had already handed in his notice at work.

I tried to pray, but I couldn't open my mouth. I tried to read my Bible, but I could only close it again. Life hurt too much for simple platitudes. I had already sustained too many broken dreams in my growing-up years, and now the same was happening. Everything I considered good was yet again being torn away.

Sadder still, I equated God with those who had harmed me as a young woman. God must be harsh because he had allowed all these things to happen. He must be spiteful because all of this felt downright mean. So I grieved, like the women of Jerusalem when they lost their pleasant homes, their livelihoods: 'Strip off your fine clothes and wrap yourselves in rags. Beat your breasts… yes, mourn' (Isaiah 32:11–13). I howled in my heart and those rags hung from my shoulders as witnesses to my grief.

There was a widow in the Bible who suffered intensely as well. Her husband had relocated her and their two sons to a foreign country. But then he died, and her sons died as well, leaving her with two foreign daughters-in-law. Broken and devastated, Naomi decided to move back home.

She tried to dissuade her daughters-in-law from following her. 'Why would you come with me?… It is more bitter for me than you, because the Lord's hand has turned against me!' (Ruth 1:11, 13). As far as Naomi was concerned, God had purposefully made all this happen. He had destroyed her. So she felt duty-bound to convince those young women that her God was in no way safe to follow. Even though they came from a culture which worshipped a god of war, which included human sacrifice, Naomi pushed them away.

One of them went back home, but the other, Ruth, stayed. She said, 'Don't urge me to leave you… Where you go I will go, and where you stay I will stay. Your people will be my people and your God my God' (Ruth 1:16). Somehow Naomi's heart caught her attention. Somehow, Naomi revealed an authentic faith, and to Ruth, this pulled at a cord in her heart. 'Your God my God.'

Not long after, one of Naomi's relatives married Ruth and she had a son. This son became a grandfather to the most famous king in Israel, King David, who lived with the same authenticity as his great-grandmother. When he went through his own intense suffering, he wrote, 'My God, my God, why have you forsaken me? Why are you so far from saving me?… But you, Lord… are my strength; come quickly to help me' (Psalm 22:1, 19). David too went to God with his hurt confusion.

How this comforted me. I wasn't in this place alone. I could awake to the fact that not understanding God is part of a process of getting to know and trust him. As I did, I could shed my rags of grief, of feeling betrayed, and clothe myself with his strength. I could get up and live. Just as God called out a third double imperative to Jerusalem, he calls out to us, 'Awake, awake, Zion, clothe yourself with strength! Put on your garments of splendour… Shake off your dust; rise up, sit enthroned, Jerusalem. Free yourself from the chains on your neck, Daughter Zion, now a captive' (Isaiah 52:1–2). God wants us to tear off every rag that symbolises our captivity, that might hold us back from following him. He wants us to put on his splendour and strength.

An elderly lady once got in touch with me, asking if she could become my fashion advisor. She assured me I needed help, and I agreed, for I had grown up poor and in a house where 'pretty' equalled 'bad'. Even now, as a liberated woman, I spent hardly anything on myself. So I gratefully accepted.

She arrived, posh shopping bags in hand, and my eyes lit up. But as she pulled out second-hand clothes, all of them 20-plus years out of date, my heart sank. I picked up a dress and held it up to my chest. 'Thanks so much for your thoughtfulness,' I said, 'but I don't think these clothes will suit me.'

The lady gave me a motherly look. 'Nonsense! I'm trying to make you look pretty. These are mine, and they are still in excellent condition. You will look nice in them.'

I gave in to her coaxing and tried one on, but the lady was shorter and heavier than me. I had to gather the dress together with a belt around my waist. 'Look in the mirror!' she exclaimed. 'You look beautiful!'

I gazed at myself, and stared at my misshaped form, with something that hung on me like a rag. A familiar painful lump appeared in my chest, one I had carried for 13 long years. For as a teenager and young adult I had been silenced. It shook me, because now I felt silenced again. I considered the choices I had.

If I took off that dress, I would hurt this well-meaning lady. If I accepted, I would hurt myself. Either decision had a negative consequence. But, if God had made me who I was, with my likes and dislikes, and this lady couldn't accept it, I shouldn't try to adjust, just to keep a false peace. Her likes and mine definitely differed, but mine merited equal value. I could be true to the person God created me to be, which meant being true to God.

I prayed for the emotional strength to remember who I am – loved, valued and precious to God. I remembered that rags were a part of my past and I didn't have to put them back on. No matter how caring and persuasive this dear lady might be, because of God's clothes and armour shielding my heart, I could say, 'Thank you for your kindness,' as I pulled the dress off over my head. I could accept my preferences and add, 'I would rather find something I like. I'm not sure what that is, but thanks for your help.'

Clothes identify us, both inside and out. If we are wearing emotional rags, God stands before us with his wonderful garments. Yet he gives us a choice. Even though his wardrobe for us will fit us perfectly, tailored to our personalities and situations in life, he still waits until we are ready. I have seen it again and again. A woman held back from leadership simply for being a woman. Her self-confidence and self-esteem end up shredded. They hang around her like rags. But then she takes the time to clothe herself with God's strength and he gives her a greater position of leadership.

A woman told that as a mother she can't have any high-level responsibilities. Her dreams and trust in others are shredded. They hang around her like rags. But then she takes the time to clothe herself with God's tenacious strength and he gives her the joy of working with thousands of children.

A woman who loses her husband to another. Her self-worth and well-being are destroyed. They hang around her like filthy rags. But she takes the time to clothe herself with the greatest strength of all – forgiveness – and God surrounds her with people who love her.

And there is more in God's wardrobe:

- He is 'clothed with **splendour and majesty**. The Lord wraps himself in **light** as with a garment' (Psalm 104:1–2).
- He has '**righteousness** [as] his belt and **faithfulness** the sash round his waist' (Isaiah 11:5).
- He has 'the helmet of **salvation** on his head; he put on garments of **vengeance** and wrapped himself in **zeal** as in a cloak' (Isaiah 59:17).

God has an amazing wardrobe, but in the list above there is one garment he does not share, and he asks us not to grab it: vengeance. 'Do not take revenge, my dear friends, but leave room for God's wrath, for it is written: "It is mine to avenge; I will repay," says the Lord' (Romans 12:19).

God knows that we will never see the entire picture in another person's life. Those who hurt us are usually hurt themselves. Those who are unkind are usually suffering somehow in their hearts. It doesn't justify them, but God understands, and he will work with them, teach them and help them, if they let him. And if they don't, he still loves them. As is always the case, both of us are precious and both of us need rescuing.

And God never gives up on us as we dither and live undecided, as we grow accustomed to our rags. He loves us that much. It is just like when I lost my engagement ring, a ruby encircled with twelve small diamonds – the first proper ring I had ever owned. First, I checked where I normally put it, on the kitchen windowsill or my dressing table. Next, I hunted all over the house, looking in every place twice, then three times, just in case.

I missed my engagement ring. It meant a lot to me. Just as it was a declaration of Derek's love for me, of his promise to marry me, it also symbolised a battle won. Derek had helped me stand up for my life. He had enabled me to escape from extreme manipulation. He had walked with me when others did their best to stop our wedding. My engagement ring symbolised freedom, hope and love.

I went to Derek at the end of the day. 'Derek, I've lost my engagement ring.' We prayed and hunted again, but we never found it.

Then six months later, I watched my teenage son lob an apple core into a bowl of peels. He missed, and it landed on the kitchen windowsill, right where I used to keep my ring. An idea popped into my head. What if my ring had somehow been knocked into a bowl of peels? Maybe it was in the compost heap behind the house.

I put on my grubbiest clothes and some work gloves, and I found a huge piece of plastic. I spread out the plastic on the grass beside the heap, and then I surveyed the heap, a hefty pile, three feet high and five feet wide. This would take me quite a while.

I grabbed a first handful of kitchen refuse and grass clippings. I fell to my knees and spread it out on the plastic sheet, sifting through it one tiny section at a time, my face close to the smelly, decomposing muck. I found nothing.

For the next two hours, I worked without a break. The compost heap grew smaller. Surely, I should have found it by now. But I decided to keep on going until every bit of the heap had been checked. Half an hour later, as I took up another handful of gooey muck, with long wriggling earthworms sliding through my fingers, I spotted my ring half-buried in the heap. It sparkled in the afternoon sun.

I shrieked with joy and grabbed it. I danced in circles with it raised in the air. 'Thank you, God!' I sang. Then I threw off my mucky work gloves and washed my ring in the rain barrel. I ran inside. 'I found it, Derek!' I cried. He embraced me in all my smelly and sweaty glory. He put that ring on my finger, for I was still his bride.

To me, the image of my ring sparkling in the compost heap symbolised my past. I had been buried. But God found me, cleaned me up and took off my rags, as he did for Jerusalem when he found her abandoned as a young woman. He said:

> I bathed you with water and washed the blood from you and put ointments on you. I clothed you with an embroidered dress and put sandals of fine leather on you. I dressed you in fine linen and covered you with costly garments. I adorned you with jewellery.
> EZEKIEL 16:9–11

God sees us in our brokenness. He sees our rags, but he isn't revulsed. Instead, we hear beautiful, comforting words: 'Do not grieve, for the joy of the Lord is your strength' (Nehemiah 8:10); 'The Lord is my strength and my defence; he has become my salvation. He is my God, and I will praise him' (Exodus 15:2). Despite the metaphorical meteors which keep knocking us down, which tear our clothes into shreds, we can move on and put on God's clothes. We can shed those rags of doubt and fear. We can live with dignity and strength.

The Bible says, 'In that day the Lord Almighty will be a glorious crown, a beautiful wreath for the remnant of his people. He will be a... source of strength to those who turn back the battle at the gate' (Isaiah 28:5–6). God gives us the strength and means to fight. As we do, he himself becomes the crown on our heads. He stands with us. He fights with us, both of us arrayed in his marvellous clothes, and together we turn back the enemy. He enables us to win.

A time to reflect

Take some time to think on Isaiah 52:1–2 once again: 'Awake, awake, Zion, clothe yourself with strength! Put on your garments of splendour... Shake off your dust; rise up, sit enthroned, Jerusalem. Free yourself from the chains on your neck, Daughter Zion.' If you feel like you can, consider the following questions:

- How does God want you to live – in rags or in his clothes? Why?
- What do you think God wants you to put on today?
- How can you make that happen?

As you are able, take some time later today to think further on these verses. Record your thoughts in your journal.

4

GOD'S FOURTH CALL: DEPART!

**Depart, depart, go out from there! Touch no unclean thing!
Come out from it and be pure.**

Isaiah 52:11

An earnest call for Jerusalem to leave behind everything which held her back. And the same earnest call comes to each of us, for we can't move on until we have let go.

Depart:
how can I let go?

**Depart, depart, go out from there! Touch no unclean thing!
Come out from it and be pure.**

One winter's night, as a teenager, a group of us drove home, down a narrow country road near where we lived. There were high snowbanks piled up on each side and hardly anyone ever travelled that road, especially at night. We approached a crossroads and saw a dark mass on the snowbank up ahead. I thought it must be a dead deer. Someone had hit the poor thing.

We drove closer. All of us cried out in alarm. A person lay there instead!

The driver skidded to a halt, and we jumped from the car. We climbed up on the snowbank and I cried out again. It was a girl. Partially dressed. Hip-hugger, bell-bottom jeans and a skimpy top. The top had slipped half off her shoulder and had gathered up around her chest. Bare skinned, she lay directly on the snow. For me, the worst part was that she looked about my age – 15. Who could have been so cruel as to dump her in the snow, in a remote place where no one would find her?

The driver picked up her hand and felt for her pulse. 'She's alive!' he said. 'We need an ambulance!'

'We need to get her off the snowbank first,' I cried. 'She will freeze to death.'

'Don't touch her,' he said. 'We don't know how she has been hurt. Run and get help.'

Some of us ran up the icy road with all our might, the car headlights showing our way. We banged on a stranger's front door, crying out in anguish for someone to open. Someone finally did, and we pointed down the road, our words coming out in a jumble.

That person ran to his telephone, and we ran back to the group. I looked at the girl. She now had a coat covering her body. The driver's coat! And he stood like a sentinel in his short-sleeved shirt.

We stayed there until an ambulance arrived, and the next day the driver told us that he had telephoned the police. Was that young girl alright? Yes, she would remain in the hospital a few days, but would make a full recovery. He also found out that she had gone to a party without telling her parents, and then had been dumped more than 50 miles from her home.

I shuddered. It could very well have been me. I too had dreamed of sneaking out and going to parties with my friends. Now this girl, without meaning to, showed me the consequences. She had made a passionate choice, followed her desires, and it had almost cost her her life.

Jerusalem experienced the same, putting feet to her passions. The account is graphic:

> You trusted in your beauty and used your fame to become a prostitute. You lavished your favours on anyone who passed by and your beauty became his… You also took the fine jewellery I gave you, the jewellery made of my gold and silver, and you made for yourself male idols and engaged in prostitution with them… And you took your sons and daughters whom you bore to me and sacrificed them as food to the idols.
> EZEKIEL 16:15, 17, 20

Because of her choices, she hurt herself and others. She left God. But God didn't remain silent in her pain, and his.

His fourth double imperative rang loud and clear. 'Depart, depart, go out from there! Touch no unclean thing! Come out from it and be pure, you who carry the articles of the Lord's house' (Isaiah 52:11). He wanted her to leave her past unwise passions and get away from those people and places that once excited her. He wanted her to come back to him, to give her heart to him in purity.

Jerusalem eventually did. Revelation 21:2 says, 'I saw the Holy City, the new Jerusalem, coming down out of heaven from God, prepared as a bride beautifully dressed for her husband.' But to get to this point, she had to let go of past passions. This is true for each one of us. Even though we know God has comforted us, woken us up and clothed us, we can still cling on to our past passions. For me, a powerful passion was survival. What I went through as a young woman was destructive, and surviving became a driving force. It dictated how I spoke, how I felt about myself and how I lived my life. Once I was set free from those who hurt me, I realised that protecting myself had become a habit and affected everyone around me, whether they were a threat or not. So to depart meant to let go of hiding from people, for that made me feel safe.

'Depart, depart,' God calls, but of all the seven double imperatives this one is still the hardest for me. The first three are precious gifts from God: his comfort, his waking me up, his dressing me – all extravagantly lavished on me. But to take a decisive step to let go of this passion was too difficult for me. I thought that if I let go of my survival mode, there would be nothing left of me. So for years I stood stuck in this place, with the fourth double imperative in front of me.

The prophet Elijah called out to those who passionately followed something other than God. He cried, 'How long will you waver between two opinions? If the Lord is God, follow him; but if Baal[7] is God, follow him' (1 Kings 18:21). I couldn't just sit on the fence, accept God's good gifts and still hang on to that which pulled me down. But hang on to it, I certainly did. I continually wept at the injustices and prayed for God to be my hitman, to get rid of those who hurt me. But this wasn't God's way. Instead, this divided my affections. It was either a Past-with-Pain or Today-with-God.

But I didn't know how to let go. I didn't feel free in my heart to move on, so God sent me examples and encouragements.

An elderly lady once stopped me on the street. I barely knew her. 'I hope you would never judge a person for what they do,' she said.

I looked at her, baffled, surprised by her directness. 'No, I would hope not either,' I said.

She took a step closer, and I took a step back. 'Most people would judge a young woman if she abandoned her baby. They would call her cruel and callous for leaving it behind. But nobody considers what she might be going through, the unbearable pressure she feels, forcing her to go against her heart.'

I nodded, feeling dread and pain. Where was this lady headed in this strange conversation? But I also understood. I might not have shared the same experience, but as a young woman I certainly experienced the trauma of troubles, and because I couldn't escape, I often wished I were dead.

That elderly lady searched my eyes and then she nodded as if I had passed a test. She said, 'When I was young, my husband's girlfriend moved into my house. Everyone told me I should leave, but my little child needed a father.

'I kept telling my husband she didn't love him, and then one day he fell ill. That woman moved out and how I thanked God. I was the one who held his hand when he died.'

I listened, blinking back tears. She paused and then said, 'People still judge me. Do you?'

'No!' I cried, deeply shaken. I couldn't grasp such pure love, such crazy selflessness in this awful love triangle. This woman chose the path she felt God wanted her to walk. Others misunderstood her and judged her, but she walked away from their criticism. She left behind her reputation. To me, she suddenly became a truly remarkable woman. She left behind a passion to be liked and respected, because she had a greater passion – love for her husband and child.

It is only when we leave one passion that we can fully follow another. And God wants us to make him our passion. He says, 'Come out from them and be separate... Touch no unclean thing, and I will receive you' (2 Corinthians 6:17). It is so simple, yet totally life-altering, for to depart means to leave the one and to join the other. It is being free to walk away.

Yet we might not want to leave. One such person, a middle-aged man, fell in love with his secretary. Instead of listening to the cries of his family and breaking off his illicit relationship, he went his own way. Several years later, he spoke of how he had missed his children's precious growing-up years and added, 'If I had worked half as hard on my first marriage as I do on my second, it would have been heaven on earth. But I didn't.'

This man had refused to depart from a path which ultimately led him through great pain, because at that moment he passionately felt it the right thing to do. The Bible says, 'The heart is deceitful above all things and beyond cure. Who can understand it?' (Jeremiah 17:9). That is why we are in such desperate need of God's help, for we can get confused by our passions and about which are the ones from which we should depart.

I grew up with a lot of anxiety, based on an unwise and passionate response of always wanting to please others. I had learned early on that I had better be perfect if I wanted to be accepted. If I failed, which I did all the time, trouble and shame came my way. People turned their backs on me, humiliated and maligned me.

After I got married, Derek often prayed for me, asking God to emotionally heal me, but the waves of crippling anxiety refused to go away and regularly washed over me. I prayed for myself as well and read the Bible, but those voices from my past kept tormenting me, telling me I was worth nothing and didn't deserve to be happy. How I wanted to fulfil God's double imperative to 'depart, depart', but I didn't know how.

One day, in tired desperation, I read a verse. It said, 'He put a new song in my mouth, a hymn of praise to our God' (Psalm 40:3). 'Dear Jesus,' I prayed, 'please give me a new song. I'm so tired of singing the old one, of not being good enough, of not pleasing people, of thinking I am a failure.'

Not long after I came upon another verse: 'Praise him with the strings' (Psalm 150:4). It felt like a command, but there were so many kinds of strings. Harps. Guitars. Piano strings. 'Okay, God,' I prayed. 'Which one?'

Later that day, a local free newspaper came through the post. I read it, hunting for second-hand furniture. Instead, I found a violin. It had been placed in the wrong section, tucked in between used sofas and chairs! 'Dear Jesus,' I prayed, 'if these are the strings you're talking about, I'll wait a week before I ring, just to make sure it's from you.'

A week later I told Derek about my prayer, and he handed me the telephone. I rang. The violin was still there. We bought it, even though I had no idea how to play it.

I found a violin book and tried to teach myself. I failed. I found a teacher, but it went no better. I had picked up bad habits and couldn't get a decent sound. I couldn't find my new song, and this shook me. How could I depart from what was old if I couldn't grasp the new? I decided to hunt for yet another teacher. This time the best one I could find.

I'm sure my second teacher took me on out of pity, even after his assessment of me: 'You sound terrible, like a screeching cat.' Then in halting English, he pronounced my verdict, 'We will have to start all over again.'

My teacher began to tear apart every bad habit I had picked up, and God used the opportunity to do the same in my life. It felt like the teacher and God were in cahoots. 'Why are you so tense?' my teacher asked. 'Beauty only comes as you relax.'

'I don't know how to relax,' I cried. 'I have to be perfect in everything I do.'

'Forget perfection,' my teacher said. 'Play with the same feeling you have towards your husband. Love. Love is *never* tense. Love creates beauty.'

I managed an uncertain nod and assured my teacher I would try. At home, I picked up my violin, but no matter how much love I tried to put into my playing, the old habits refused to budge. I stomped around the house in confused frustration. I wanted to throw the violin out the window. 'This isn't a new song,' I cried out. 'This is demolition.'

Derek, however, watched me and grinned. 'Keep going,' he said. 'I think you've finally met your match. God is taking you somewhere.'

I glared at Derek, but I picked up my violin. I concentrated on playing just one note, playing it for hours on end, practising the new techniques I had learned. I practised until I got it to sound as it should. It took months, but a new song began to sing in my heart as well, one which said, 'I am loved and precious. I am safe in Jesus.' God used a violin to begin healing my heart and mind, causing me to become passionate about what God thought of me and to believe him with all my heart.

And what of those destructive memories from the past? The terrors they instilled are slowly disappearing. Occasionally, they still creep up on me and pounce, knocking me down. But I am learning that as soon as they pop into my mind, I can take them to God and leave them there. Sure, it takes me a while to regain equilibrium, for an injustice will always be an injustice, a wrong will always be a wrong. But God has things in control. I am free to leave them in his capable hands and know that in his good time he will sort things out. Then I sing my new song again, that I am his beloved.

God doesn't leave us to figure out this process of departing by ourselves. 'The One who breaks open the way will go up before them; they will break through the gate and go out. Their King will pass through before them, the Lord at their head' (Micah 2:13). God will do what is necessary to set us free from hurtful passions that imprison us. He will break down gates, closed doors, barred ways, so we can depart. He guides us in those first fragile steps, for it takes time to let memories, old passions and people go. As we see God in all his splendour, saving us, our love for him will grow.

There was a man in the Bible who suffered intensely. His brothers sold him into slavery and then he met them many years later. Yet he could say, 'You intended to harm me, but God intended it for good to accomplish what is now being done, the saving of many lives' (Genesis 50:20). He could depart from old feelings of anger and bitterness, of unforgiveness and revenge, because God showed him a bigger picture.

God is like that. He 'breaks down gates of bronze and cuts through bars of iron' (Psalm 107:16). Just as he enabled Joseph, and that elderly woman in a love-triangle, to find him – a far better and pure passion – he will also help us. We can all follow God in his cry to 'depart, depart'.

God is constantly attentive to our passionate hearts. He 'will save his people on that day as a shepherd saves his flock. They will sparkle in his land like jewels in a crown' (Zechariah 9:16). Regardless of how long it takes, and wherever we are in the process, God enables us to follow him. This delights him so much that he passionately places us like jewels in his crown.

A time to reflect

Pause to think about God's fourth call: 'Depart, depart, go out from there! Touch no unclean thing! Come out from it and be pure, you who carry the articles of the Lord's house' (Isaiah 52:11). Cconsider the following questions:

- Is there a passion holding you back in life?
- How can God help you break out?
- How can you make God a passion in your life?

When you have a spare moment, continue to think about Isaiah 52:11. Record your thoughts in your journal.

Depart: am I really free?

Depart, depart, go out from there! Touch no unclean thing! Come out from it and be pure.

As our hearts begin to blossom with love for God, our past passions may obstinately call us back, like abandoned lovers or aggrieved taskmasters. Just when we think everything is okay, we hear those voices from our past, because we trained ourselves to stay attuned. We cared for them and acknowledged how they made us feel. They gave us an identity; passionate desires, good or bad, are like that – they define us. They direct our life.

It happened to Jerusalem. At first, she was God's beloved, but she left him for other lovers. Next, she was a broken-hearted woman, but God told her, 'Although you have been forsaken and hated, with no one travelling through, I will make you the everlasting pride and the joy of all generations' (Isaiah 60:15). Through her passions she had acquired an unwelcome identity, but God still saw her as his beloved. God sees us in the same way, despite those passions which might have redefined us.

So, God calls out to us, 'Depart, depart, go out from there! Touch no unclean thing' (Isaiah 52:11). He wants us to let go of old definitions of ourselves, but there is a powerful emotion which could hold us back – helplessness. This helplessness can come from feeling that leaving a passionate desire, no matter how much we might love it or be revulsed by it, means we lose our identity. It is what keeps us together. So we literally can't take another step.

When a dear relative died, her executor asked each of us to choose something of her belongings. I very much liked a two-foot-high green vase that this relative had kept in her hallway, and the executor offered to package it and send it over. It arrived a month later, but when the delivery man handed the box to me, it made a slight noise.

I shook it and heard glass rattling inside. 'It's broken!' I cried.

The delivery man shrugged his shoulders and told me in a matter-of-fact voice the procedure for getting a remuneration for broken parcels. I stared at him, incredulous, but feeling totally helpless. I had so desired that vase, for it would tangibly remind me of my precious relative and how she had loved and respected me when others hadn't. But now it was broken. Something irreversible had just happened and I could do nothing about it.

My deep desire to surround myself with positive memories of love had been shattered. I stood by the open front door watching the delivery man climb back into his van and drive away. What could I do? Someone else had yet again broken something I deeply valued that would remind me of what I wanted to be – loved. Should I return it? Throw it away? Keep it? It was irreplaceable.

I finally opened it on the dining room table and stared at the multitude of jagged pieces. Did love always end up this way? Broken? I suddenly experienced another powerful passion – the incredible desire to be whole. All my growing-up years, I had suffered shame, been silenced and been robbed of respect. Yet how I clung on to a semblance of togetherness. But now this vase proved to me, yet again, that somehow beautiful things always get broken. Nothing I could do would undo this fact. So I put the box aside. I could do nothing else.

Over the next months, however, God began to work in my heart. I didn't need a vase to remember this relative. My identity didn't depend on the sweet memories of someone who loved me. Sure, I was deeply thankful, but my identity didn't rest on her opinion of me. And as for my brokenness, it was a fact, but this didn't mean that God loved me less. To him, I was still beautiful, still his precious daughter, still wonderful.

One rainy school holiday a few months later, my young son and I opened that box again. We spread out the pieces on the dining room table and studied them. We had a choice: throw it away or fix it. 'Would you like to help me rebuild this?' I asked my son. 'It's almost like a 3D jigsaw puzzle.'

He nodded and we began matching pieces together. We glued them and wound tape around them to hold them in place. We took breaks, dipping biscuits in cups of milk, discussing our next move. Finally, three days later, we finished.

We stood back and studied the vase with its white jagged lines zigzagging across the surface. God never intended for this vase to get smashed. It happened through someone else's carelessness. But that didn't mean it should end up on the rubbish heap, just as my passion to be whole didn't depend on not being broken. My passionate desire to remember those who were kind to me didn't need perfect reminders.

So I filled my dear relative's vase with dried flowers and put it in a place I could see. It is still there as a constant reminder, lest I forget that it is God, who 'heals the broken-hearted and binds up their wounds' (Psalm 147:3), who gives us our identity. He helps the helpless and enables us to move on. Sure, white break lines might criss-cross our hearts, but God enables us to depart from the power of old passions and find freedom in him.

There is a Bible passage that has helped me recently, as I stepped away from yet another passion, a job I had for six fulfilling years. After Jesus died, two women stood by his tomb. They wept for him, a man who had comforted them, who had helped them wake up and who had introduced them to God's wonderful wardrobe. But now he was gone.

Suddenly, however, two angels appeared and said, 'Why do you look for the living among the dead? He is not here; he has risen!' (Luke

24:5–6). Those angels shared an insight with those women, one so simple, yet so obvious. The passion to be with Jesus, good as it was, now had become an old passion. Those women could let it go and begin to seek this new Jesus, a risen and eternal one. 'So the women hurried away from the tomb, afraid yet filled with joy' (Matthew 28:8). We can do the same, letting go of our past and its definition of us. We can embrace God's new.

When we do this, an amazing thing happens. We find that helplessness leaves. We once again find our voice and our identity. The shame we feared from departing from those attachments, from exposing to everyone that we were nothing without them, disappears as well. Like those two women at the tomb, our living Jesus can become our new and permanent passion. And he will give us life.

A young woman once told me her story of a passion that almost ended her. Let's call her Karen.

I believed we were meant to be together, and I wanted to marry this man. However, we both sensed from God that we should wait. It was a difficult delay, but I felt it wouldn't be permanent. We had both professed our love for each other, and I trusted this man. I believed it would all work out.

Whatever this man understood when God spoke to us both, he knew I believed that we were still in a relationship. But a few months later, I caught him with another woman. It broke my heart. I confronted him, but he told me nothing was going on, that is, until he realised I had seen them.

I died in my heart. Food tasted like sawdust. I couldn't sleep. I withdrew. I lived with terror and memory loss. Flashbacks tormented me. It took almost a year to laugh again, seven years before I felt I had recovered from those severe internal injuries.

Yet the hardest part in it all was my relationship with God. I had always talked to God and wanted to obey him, and I had felt convinced that God wanted me to marry this man. Instead, this man would be marrying another. I felt such shame at having gotten it wrong and I felt duped. How could I ever listen to God's guidance for me again? I was not trustworthy.

But the only way out is through. I began to live and breathe Psalm 23:

> The Lord is my shepherd, I lack nothing. He makes me lie down in green pastures, he leads me beside quiet waters, he refreshes my soul. He guides me along the right path for his name's sake. Even though I walk through the darkest valley, I will fear no evil, for you are with me; your rod and your staff, they comfort me. You prepare a table before me in the presence of my enemies. You anoint my head with oil; my cup overflows. Surely your goodness and love will follow me all the days of my life, and I will dwell in the house of the Lord forever.

It wasn't just something I read; it kept me alive when I wanted to give up. One night especially, as I slept outside, I woke up in a terror. I often did. But as I looked at the stars in the universe above me, Orion the Hunter directly over me, I had the strongest sense of God's vastness. The very God who had created those stars was carrying me.

I felt reassured that God had spoken to me, but the man I loved could choose to do what God asked, or not. All these years later,

> I am grateful to God. I don't understand why it happened and I wouldn't want it repeated, but for all my sorrow, I believe God protected me.

God enabled Karen to leave her feelings of helplessness, of feeling trapped, and God can do the same for us. We might have preferred another storyline for our lives, of being loved and accepted by those we love, but God says to us, 'Do not be afraid, for I am with you' (Isaiah 43:5). Others might reject us, but God never will. We can depart from the shattered identities that come through broken relationships or troubles. We can walk with God into a new kind of freedom.

If we read Isaiah 43:1 and put our names in place instead, we can see what God thinks of us:

> But now, this is what the Lord says – he who created you, _____ [your name], he who formed you, _____ [your name]: 'Do not fear, for I have redeemed you; I have summoned you by name: you are mine.'

We are secure in God's hands. For with God, nothing can stop us from walking with him – no passion, no person, not even our feelings of helplessness. Nothing can stop him from helping us, and him becoming our passion in life.

For many years as a young adult, I worked at home, long hours, six days a week and without any pay. We could still barely make ends meet. Yet I passionately believed that if I worked harder and did a better job, I could rescue the situation. I poured out my life, but others made poor choices and we ended up homeless. After a while, I didn't even bother bringing up my own dreams. I felt faceless, voiceless, identity-less. Then one day I was asked to go and pick up some car parts.

I packed a couple of sandwiches for the 200-mile round trip and spread out a road map on the front seat beside me. But halfway there I had read the map incorrectly. I had taken a wrong turn and ended up on a winding road with no place to turn around for miles. I chided myself for my carelessness. Now I would be arriving late.

Fifteen minutes later I found a place to turn, another fifteen to get back and continue in the right direction again. I drove a couple of miles and entered a residential area, where I looked around me in horror. Telephone poles lay on the ground like pick-up sticks. There were no cars, no people, no movement. A tornado had just passed through, following the road.

I drove along in shocked silence, not knowing what else to do. Then a thought flashed into my mind. If I hadn't gotten lost, I would have been hit by that tornado. I probably would have died. God had kept me from going the right way, by allowing me to misread the map. (I later learned that no one had been hurt by that tornado.)

I shuddered, but then burst out singing from Handel's Messiah: 'For the Lord God omnipotent reigneth.' God had just saved me. He also conveyed a message I would otherwise not have believed. He used an extreme situation to get my attention. He wanted me to know how much he loved me. He wanted me to understand that I had great worth, and he was the one who protected me. He wanted me to know that I wasn't helpless. If other people had a certain view of me, that wasn't God's view. He had given me strength and dignity, and that was a fact.

God points out our misguided and wrong passions, and tells us we have the freedom to depart from them. My friend Becks shared a story of what this looked like for her.

I had recently moved back from overseas and began to seek registration as an accredited counsellor. I had already worked part-time in the field for 15 years and now I began taking the courses necessary to fulfil the requirements. Usually, I found it enjoyable to learn, but this time I found the classes erratic and stressful. I began to question my motivation.

I realised that I was afraid to let it go. I was attached to my job and proud of it. Counselling had become a part of my identity and I felt I wouldn't count for much if I didn't continue in my career. But maybe I needed to let it go and trust God for who I was.

I looked deeper into my heart, and I realised more than anything else I wanted to have Jesus as I grew older. A verse in the Bible guided me: 'Take delight in the Lord, and he will give you the desires of your heart' (Psalm 37:4).

I hadn't thought much of the desires of my heart for the 20 years I spent raising my children, working and all the house moves we had to make. But now counselling began to take that place, and I knew I could only have one master in my life. Would I decide to continue with my accreditation, or could I step away from my career and trust the Lord for my future? I felt the Lord was offering me a choice.

I chose to trust, but trembled at the prospect, at the huge sacrifice I would make. But God showed such gentleness. The more I sought him, the more he became the desire of my heart. He helped me let go, and I am so thankful to him.

God's fourth precious call is all about having a pure and devoted heart towards God, about being able to depart from passions which keep us from him. In every situation in our lives, in every passion we experience, we have permission to leave them behind, no matter what anyone says, no matter how it defines our identity. We have permission to walk away and choose God, for we are in safe hands.

The Bible says, 'Who shall separate us from the love of Christ? Shall trouble or hardship or persecution or famine or nakedness or danger or sword?… No, in all these things we are more than conquerors through him who loved us' (Romans 8:35, 37). Nothing can keep us apart from God's heart for us. *Nothing*.

A time to reflect

Take some time to think about Isaiah 52:11 once again: 'Depart, depart, go out from there! Touch no unclean thing! Come out from it and be pure, you who carry the articles of the Lord's house.' Cconsider these following questions:

- Do you feel helpless in some situation in your life?
- How can God help you leave behind the grip it has on you?
- How would you describe freedom in all of this?

If you are able, keep thinking on Isaiah 52:11. Record your thoughts in your journal.

5

GOD'S FIFTH CALL: BUILD UP!

Build up, build up, prepare the road! Remove the obstacles out of the way of my people.
Isaiah 57:14

God called his beloved Jerusalem to himself, desiring a relationship with her. We too can experience this precious relationship by drawing close to him.

Build up:
can I hear God?

Build up, build up, prepare the road! Remove the obstacles out of the way of my people.

If you have ever climbed a mountain, you will know that the first peak you see isn't necessarily the top of that mountain. It is only the first stage in getting there, and when you finally reach that first lesser summit, you might just catch a glimpse of the final peak high up in the clouds. In between there may still be lesser peaks.

This is also true as we walk with God through his seven double imperatives. With each new one we think we have made it, but God shows us yet another. Even though we have been comforted, are awake to what is going on, are wearing God's clothes and as a result have found the strength to leave old passions behind, there is yet more.

God calls out a fifth double imperative: 'Build up, build up, prepare the road! Remove the obstacles out of the way of my people' (Isaiah 57:14). For Jerusalem, this meant that God had a job for her, albeit a strange one for his beloved. He asks her to build a road!

We know that this is our job as well, but what does this mean? We can only know if we listen to him. But how do we do that when God is in heaven, and we are down here on earth?

When I asked my friend Karen that same question, this is what she said:

I grew up knowing the Bible, yet the first time I heard God speak was in a friend's back garden. I was a student at university and didn't want to be there. I had just gone through a broken engagement, and I felt so far away from home and so miserable.

I can't remember why, but we were reading Isaiah 54:11–14: 'Afflicted city, lashed by storms and not comforted, I will rebuild you with stones of turquoise, your foundations with lapis lazuli. I will make your battlements of rubies, your gates of sparkling jewels… In righteousness you will be established; tyranny will be far from you; you will have nothing to fear.' Then suddenly, like an arrow to my heart, I saw a promise that things would change, a promise that I would get rebuilt. I turned a corner that day.

These verses have become pivotal in my life. Every time there has been a 'turning of the tide' in a significant life battle, these verses come back to me. Over the last 20 years I have written six different dates by those verses, where God turned the tide in my life.

Next, I began desiring to hear God's voice in a new way. I wanted a relationship with him, but I often found reading the Bible challenging. I couldn't figure out what God was saying. So I prayed, 'God, I'm not clever enough to get what's in your word. Can you talk to me more normally, like people talk to each other?'

Then, in another life battle, Isaiah 54 came to me yet again. I trusted it, and asked God if he could speak through a picture. I suddenly felt overwhelmed by a scene from a fairy tale, of a princess changing in appearance and light shooting from her fingertips and face. I also had the impression of a voice saying, 'I will make you so well that light will physically shine out of you.'

I laughed, as I realised I had probably been watching too many movies. But I already knew that I trusted those verses from Isaiah, that restoration and being filled with light were part of God's character. I said, 'God, I believe you. Thank you. I look forward to that day. Also, if you put those images in my mind and you are speaking, please tell a stranger so I can be sure I didn't just imagine it.'

Three days later people started saying, 'You look radiant. There is a lot of light coming out of you!'

Later, I went to a conference and a team of three people prayed for me. They sat there, not speaking to each other, writing in notebooks, asking God how he had made me and all the things he loved about me. Then they shared what they had heard. ALL three had images of me being filled with light, and one woman had the picture of the very same princess radiating light! I burst into tears. God *had* spoken to me. Me.

My friend Karen heard from God. He spoke to her in various ways. He comforted her and gave her dignity. But she had to listen, and that is often the hard part. Listening requires space, time and availability. It requires giving proper attention and weight to the speaker. As we come to the fifth call and stand before a road that God calls us to build, we must learn to listen to him carefully.

Jesus put it so well. He said, 'My sheep listen to my voice; I know them, and they follow me' (John 10:27). Jesus wants to lead us in life. He speaks, but we are the ones who make the decision to listen and follow. It would be impossible to build this road if we didn't. Yet you might feel like shrugging your shoulders. How does this actually happen in reality? How do we know that we are hearing God's voice, and not our own passions or inner voice?

This is my story of how I learned to differentiate.

As a 25-year-old and in my third year at Bible college, a missionary came to speak at one of our student chapel meetings. He challenged us with Bible verses and stories to give financially to missions. He encouraged us to be bold and ask God for how much to give. Until that point, my prayers to God had mainly been ones of survival, for money to live, for escape from continued severe manipulation and how to cope with singleness.

Now this missionary speaker was asking me to go deeper, to give for the survival of others. It touched my heart, and I raised my hand at the end of chapel saying I would give to a missionary organisation. Afterwards I hurried to the library and opened my Bible. Maybe God would tell me how much to give and to whom. He had never spoken to me like this.

I had no sense of what I should do, so I did nothing. Yet the feeling that I should give kept nagging at me. Three months later I knew I had better do something and I would have to figure it out on my own.

I looked around me at the people in Bible college. One of my teachers had recently come back from the mission field for a year of furlough. I would give my gift to him and his wife.

I went to the bank and withdrew $40, even though I knew I would have to scrape by for a while. I put it in an envelope and wondered how to address it. On the spur of the moment, I wrote the wife's name down. I would give it to the teacher the next day in class and he could pass it on to her.

How I hoped I was doing the right thing. The missionaries might be quite well-off and then I would be the one in need. But I had made a promise in chapel, and I wanted to get it off my chest.

Three days later I received a letter from that wife. It went something like this:

Dear Eva, thank you for your gift. I can't express enough what it means to me personally, that you chose to send your gift to me. I have been struggling lately. We left everything to serve God, to go overseas as missionaries, and when we came back it felt like he had abandoned us. Things have been very tough, and to top it off we ran out of food. We only had two slices of bread left in the cupboard to feed our little children.

Then your letter came, not to my husband, but to me. It was as if God was letting me know he hadn't forgotten me. He was showing me he has everything under control. As you can imagine, we went straight to the store and bought the food we needed.

Thank you for listening to God.

Your sister in Christ

I sat down hard. I had heard from God without even knowing it. He had been with me all along without me even being aware. I had done what he wanted without recognising him. I laughed. I was delighted. I felt so at one with God. I had just become a part of an amazing God-story. But now I also had clues as to what God sounded like.

I studied each moment of the process, remembered each feeling. Yes, God's voice was different from the other ones I had heard, when my mind had been filled up with the voices of those who controlled me – loud ones, cold ones and syrupy-sweet manipulative ones.

God's voice, however, felt like a gentle breeze, like a breath, by putting an idea in my head. But it felt like a nudge as well, like a gentle push on my shoulder, enabling me to follow him. 'Go to the bank.' 'Write her name down on the envelope.' 'Give your letter to them as soon as you can.' He was right there with me! Together we gave hope to that precious woman.

Recently, Derek, I and our two younger children went to a county fair. One of the events was a sheepdog trial, and we watched an owner with her dogs. It amazed me to see how they took on the challenge to herd a dozen ungainly geese. They worked together as a team.

Hundreds of us stood outside a roped-off area watching those wilful geese, as they got ushered up steps, through a tunnel and down a slide into a paddling pool. Children cheered. Everyone clapped. The noise could be heard all around the fair. Yet that sheepdog heard nothing but his owner's voice. He followed every call and point of the hand. He stopped when told. He ran in the right direction. The owner gave undivided attention to her dog. They worked together as a team.

The owner then explained how she trained her sheepdogs. She started when they were pups, bonding with them and developing trust. Then when they were around a year old, when they were emotionally mature, she began to train. But it took a lot of time and patience. Each sheepdog had to learn to follow her commands, and often it proved difficult. At the beginning, those young dogs couldn't resist the temptation to scatter instead of gather. But they soon learned to trust and obey.

The same is true for us. It takes time to develop this careful listening to God. Jesus, through his Holy Spirit, teaches us how to listen well. He shows us how to follow him. He shows that he is trustworthy and worth following.

In all my journey of walking with God, it has always boiled down to this: knowing that he is trustworthy; knowing that he never lies; knowing that he always has our best interests at heart; and even in the ups and downs of life, in the extreme challenges and joys, knowing that he still speaks. He wants to communicate with us. Just as he promised Jerusalem, he promises to us, 'Whether you turn to the right or to the left, your ears will hear a voice behind you, saying, "This is the way; walk in it"' (Isaiah 30:21). And how he desires for us to pay careful attention.

Communication requires speaking and hearing. It is two-way. For a healthy relationship, it also requires trust, taking the speaker and listener seriously. The Bible says, 'Trust in the Lord with all your heart and lean not on your own understanding; in all your ways submit to him, and he will make your paths straight' (Proverbs 3:5–6). Trust is a prerequisite for following God.

Sadly, for Jerusalem, her story was different. An enemy army overtook her city and set up a puppet ruler within her gates. But someone local resented this and murdered that man. Suddenly darkness and fear descended on Jerusalem and her people. They feared for their lives, expecting heavy reprisals and more destruction. So they ran to the prophet Jeremiah and asked if he could inquire of God. They wanted to hear God's voice amid their trauma. They needed to know what to do.

Jeremiah prayed and God spoke: 'Do not be afraid of the king of Babylon, whom you now fear. Do not be afraid of him, declares the Lord, for I am with you and will save you and deliver you from his hands' (Jeremiah 42:11). He comforted them. He opened their eyes to his perspective. He asked them to put on strength and courage, making it possible to depart from unhelpful passions and turn their hearts towards him.

But the people responded, 'You are lying!' (Jeremiah 43:2). The facts didn't add up. God must be wrong. They had better run away to Egypt.

Jeremiah tried to stop them, saying: 'You made a fatal mistake when you sent me to the Lord your God and said, "Pray to the Lord our God for us; tell us everything he says and we will do it." I have told you today, but you still have not obeyed the Lord your God in all he sent me to tell you' (Jeremiah 42:20–21). That one decision to reject God's voice cost them their lives. Most of them died in Egypt. They fell into the trap of not trusting God.

It is a scary thing to neglect God's voice. I have done it often enough, thinking things through rationally and forgetting that my finite mind can't grasp the big picture God has for me. Suddenly, God's double imperative to remove the obstacles makes sense, for part of building a road is getting rid of those things that trip us up – the potholes. 'Build up, build up, prepare the road! Remove the obstacles out of the way of my people' (Isaiah 57:14) .

Now, here it is good to discover that potholes are different from passions. God calls us to depart from passions, to walk away from them.

But with potholes, they must be filled in. These are those obstacles that keep tripping us up and hindering us in our walk with God, and they can be emotional, mental, spiritual or physical. For me, they are mainly survival responses to painful memories. Other times it is a character issue that causes me to stumble in my walk with God.

So coming upon potholes can feel uncomfortable or painful, yet God helps us identify them, for that is the first part of, 'Build up! Build up!' But just as passions will rear their heads, so potholes open up like bottomless pits, and we need God's voice, his guidance to understand them and deal with them.

I so often fail in this area, for God will identify a pothole, but I think, 'Nope, that isn't really a problem in my life.' Or, 'I've already dealt with that!' And I fall in headfirst.

After Derek and I had been married 26 years, I was asked to give a short talk at a conference. In my heart I had walked with God and sought his help to get away from the emotional effects of metaphorical meteor strikes in my life. But as I stood at the front, a PowerPoint presentation behind me, a movement caught my eye. It was the exact same movement someone had made when they were angry with me. A flood of horror surged into my heart. Then the person looked up. He even looked like that person, down to the rage that simmered in his eyes.

I froze, even though I knew that I had done nothing wrong. My mouth went dry. I couldn't speak. I wanted to disappear into the floor. I couldn't even ask for a cup of water so I could continue speaking. How could I? Suddenly I was that helpless young woman once again, with no rights, and I plummeted into a pothole, literally unable to move.

I finally managed to bark out instructions for people to get into discussion groups, and as they did, I began to shake. I turned around and steadied myself. What was going on? This had never happened to me before. But neither had I met someone who personified this person so well. I cried out for God to help me, and a few minutes later I could stumble through the rest of my presentation. But I couldn't join in with the rest of the conference. I fled the auditorium and sat in a back room, alone, trembling, for several hours. I knew people would miss me and ask where I was, but this wasn't a time to put on a brave face. I had to sort this one out.

In the silence of that room, I stared out of the window, and a song came to mind about God being my father. I began to sing it in jagged whispers, again and again. It washed my heart and I remembered... *God* is my Father, my good Father. He is my comforter, my protector. He is the one who holds me safe. The Bible says, 'Surely he will save you from the fowler's snare and from the deadly pestilence. He will cover you with his feathers, and under his wings you will find refuge; his faithfulness will be your shield and rampart' (Psalm 91:3–4). God wanted me to listen to him, not the memory that pushed me into a snare, an agonising pothole where I again believed that this person was more powerful than God. Those shouting memories had no right to be there because now I knew they weren't true. I asked God to fill that pothole up with himself.

About a year later, I was going through another situation where someone tried to silence me. I cried out like a person suffocating for air. It brought back painful memories of when I was a young woman and the pain was so great I could tell no one in my local church. I remained trapped in a pothole where I once again felt I had no voice or the right to stand up for myself.

Yet one Sunday after the morning service a woman came up to me. 'Eva,' she said, 'I have something for you.' She pointed to some words she had written in a notebook. 'Fear not. Have faith. 'Tis I who lead the way.'[8] She looked me in the face. 'I feel like God wants me to show you these words. Somehow you are going through a tough time.'

I looked at the woman, trying to control my emotions. God had sent her to comfort me, and she didn't even know why. Through her God showed me he had everything in hand, and this was the path I needed to walk. Yes, it was dark, but God was there, speaking to me, pulling me out of that gaping pothole. Again, I asked him to fill it up with himself.

King David said, 'He lifted me out of the slimy pit, out of the mud and mire; he set my feet on a rock and gave me a firm place to stand' (Psalm 40:2). Whatever is tripping us up, hindering our walk with God, he is there sorting it out. We can learn to listen to God and trust him. Through him, those potholes can close as we let him into our lives. He smooths them away.

God is so very good. He doesn't leave us there. His promises are sure, for he 'redeems your life from the pit and crowns you with love and compassion' (Psalm 103:4). He retrieves us from every pothole that swallows us up. He fills them up with himself. Because of him, we receive yet another jewel in our crown – his forever compassion and love.

A time to reflect

Take some time to think again on, 'Build up, build up, prepare the road! Remove the obstacles out of the way of my people' (Isaiah 57:14). Ponder the questions below:

- What are some potholes in your life, things that trip you up?
- Consider one of them. What do you think God is saying to you?
- What are some Bible promises which reveal God's heart for you?

Pause to think about this verse throughout the day. Record your thoughts in your journal.

Build up: what about my heart?

Build up, build up, prepare the road! Remove the obstacles out of the way of my people.

G od calls us to 'Build up, build up,' yet you might be wondering where this road leads. For Jerusalem and for us, it leads to God. It is that simple.

Just before he gave his fifth double imperative, God called out, 'But whoever takes refuge in me will inherit the land and possess my holy mountain' (Isaiah 57:13). The link between God and Jerusalem, his city on his holy mountain, is a heart road. It is our link as well, and it is such an essential road that God gives further instructions on how to repair it.

Pothole-filling is raised to another level when God talks about our heart attitudes. He says, 'I live in a high and holy place, but also with the one who is contrite and lowly in spirit' (Isaiah 57:15). When the potholes spring from our heart, building this road is more than just asking God to fill them in; it becomes a joint effort, a collaboration with God.

We might not think of being contrite or lowly as essential pothole-filling qualities, and they might not even be a part of our vocabulary. But our heart attitude towards God will determine how this road is fixed. Sure, we can listen to him, yet we might be correcting him all the time, telling him how the job should be done. Or we might be folding our arms across our chest, saying, 'God, you have this all wrong. These potholes are who I am. Just leave them alone.'

God, however, calls us to take a next step because he knows how important it is to build up our hearts, that part of our morals, emotions and character which is distinctive to us. It would be all too easy to compare ourselves to others and tell God, 'They live with their potholes quite well. Why do I have to work on mine?' But a contrite and lowly heart enables us to let go and build with God as he knows best.

As we willingly take this next step in letting him have his way in our hearts, we begin to see that this too is part of the process of healing. S contrite person is someone who recognises their personal weaknesses and takes ownership. A lowly person is someone who lives with an attitude of humility. Both are essential for God to heal us.

Yet often these potholes only open up when we are put under pressure. If life is straightforward, with no stresses and grief, we may well find it easy to be kind, generous and tolerant. But add in stresses and griefs and the cracks will appear. It happened to me when I went for a walk one day. A stranger stopped me. But her first question wasn't 'How are you?'; it was 'Are you a Christian?'

I gawked. 'Yes,' I said, surprised by the way she started the conversation. 'I go to a church.'

'Ah!' this woman said, a look of incredulity on her face. 'Your Jesus, you know, he isn't a god. Let me tell you, gods don't die. They are eternal. They are nothing more than light, or the air around us. They are everywhere, but nowhere.'

I looked at the person, unsure how to answer. If I wanted to get on her good side, I would have to agree and conform to peace-at-all-costs. If I was content to irritate her, I would have to tell her what I believed. Yet I struggled. The past again reared its head and I so wanted to be accepted, and that familiar character flaw appeared yet again. I felt shame at being me, of having my own beliefs.

I cried out to Jesus silently. 'What should I do?' A thought came to mind. 'Don't be shamed. Just tell her what I have done for you.'

I smiled. 'I love Jesus. He is wonderful. Did you know he has literally saved me a number of times? I should be dead.'

This woman looked at me with a mixture of pity and disdain. She smirked, and suddenly I knew what I had to do. There was no foundation for a friendship here. I had opened my heart in a friendly sort of way, and she had become a judge, deciding how I should live my life. The only way this person would have been pleased was if I cast aside my beliefs and accepted hers.

It was time to move on. I bid the person goodbye and walked away. Yet I marvelled that in such a short space of time a heart pothole opened up in front of me. Yes, there were good character traits, like civility, respect and friendliness, but there was also an inordinate fear of disappointing others. It came from my past, and even though I had brought the memories to God, and he was healing them, now it had reared its head again. An excessive desire to please. A driven peace-at-all-costs attitude.

Jesus, however, was my great encouragement. He too was put into extreme situations, yet he was able to remain true to God and himself. When he went out alone into the desert, he was hungry and tired. He was cold. The devil used this opportune moment to entice the Lord of the universe to fall for him, to do what he wanted. The devil purposefully prodded Jesus, trying to make a pothole and push him in.

Jesus willingly stood firm. He understood what was happening and said, 'Away from me, Satan! For it is written: "Worship the Lord your God, and serve him only"' (Matthew 4:10). Jesus didn't worry about his reputation with the devil or care if the devil liked him. He stood firm and broke off the conversation. If Jesus could do that, so could I. I didn't have to remain in harmful relationships, just because people demanded it or tried to manipulate me into it.

God knows that as we walk through life, unexpected potholes will appear, of our making or that of others. Even though these can be painful or embarrassing, God uses them for good. As we recognise them, we can willingly work with God in doing something about them. And God constantly encourages us, reminding us that, 'The Lord himself goes before you and will be with you; he will never leave you nor forsake you. Do not be afraid; do not be discouraged' (Deuteronomy 31:8).

My friend, let's call her Jasmin, told me how God met her in her troubles and helped her fill those potholes which others had dug along her path.

I was only a child when my father died, but I wouldn't allow myself to cry. My mother was distressed, and I didn't want to add to her grief. Yet somehow everyone seemed to overlook me, and no one thought to hug me. I ended up caring for my younger siblings, and I learned not to ask for help. It became a natural way of life.

Yet there came a time when I did cry out for help. I had never experienced bullying as a child, but in my workplace I did. I felt so desperate and tried to talk with my boss, but instead of being listened to and my pain acknowledged, this person rebuffed me. I was even told there was something wrong with me and that I should stop complaining. And this person instructed me not to tell anyone else.

It almost destroyed me. My sense of personal freedom and confidence went out the window. I went into shock. I felt alone, as if no one could protect me. I felt emotionally unsafe. It was even harder than when my father died.

But I couldn't leave my job immediately. So, I went straight to God. I survived by spending time with him. Yet it wasn't easy.

How does a person who feels so insecure find their security in an unseen God?

I began reading my Bible, especially Isaiah 54. It talked about a hurting Jerusalem, and I identified with her:

'Afflicted city, lashed by storms and not comforted.' How I related.

'I will rebuild you with stones of turquoise, your foundations with lapis lazuli' (v. 11). I started crying. God would rebuild me – this was a promise – not just with rocks, but with precious stones.

'If anyone does attack you, it will not be my doing; whoever attacks you will surrender to you' (v. 15). I cried again. Yet another promise. God was involved in my situation, and I was safe with him. He planned to do something, not necessarily that minute, that day or that week, but in his time. I felt so comforted, because God was in control, and he would bring me through.

God did do something. Not long after, everyone who had hurt me left their jobs. And even though those were by far the hardest days in my life, I learned a great lesson – that all of us need to be understood by at least one person in our lives. When people pour out their hearts to me, I really listen, even if I haven't experienced their grief. I give them my attention and acknowledge the authenticity of their pain. I care for them like God cares for me.

Jasmin suffered with intense feelings of abandonment and betrayal, but God helped her. Together they filled up those places where muddy potholes grabbed at her feet. God gave her promises and she willingly listened to them. She believed them, knowing that God would enable her to move on in their journey together. Jasmin displayed a deep humility towards God, one where she knew that without him, she would not have made it. But with him, she did.

God is like that. He knows us intimately and he is with us when these potholes surface. But as Jasmine shared, they can almost kill us, especially if others try to drag us into them. It is in situations like this where the account of Jesus in the desert helps us. Jasmin couldn't tell her unkind colleagues, 'Away from me, Satan.' But God did. He moved them on. Although, it is good to remember that God loved Jasmin's oppressors as well.

Thankfully, like Jerusalem and Jasmin, we can turn to God. He speaks tenderly to us, 'Shake off your dust; rise up, sit enthroned, Jerusalem. Free yourself from the chains on your neck' (Isaiah 52:2). Even though we might encounter many potholes, God gives us the strength to fill them in. If we fall in, he helps us climb out.

No matter what has happened to us or what we have done, the potholes that appear in our lives can be closed. King David said, 'My sacrifice, O God, is a broken spirit; a broken and contrite heart you, God, will not despise' (Psalm 51:17). And it begins with a contrite and lowly heart.

As a 30-year-old, after I was finally able to escape from severe manipulation, God continued helping me fill in unseen potholes. It started by setting healthy boundaries. But as the years ticked by, they became too rigid, and I dug another two – oversensitivity and intolerance. If someone crossed a boundary, it triggered a fear that yet again I might fall into another oppressive trap. I automatically overreacted. I couldn't just kindly mention for that person to back off; instead I got deeply upset, and sadly this included my reactions to Derek.

We worked from home and had three small children by then. I felt exhausted and needed space, so Derek encouraged me to lie down for a rest. He would take over. But a few minutes later he opened the bedroom door. He handed me a sheet of paper. 'Eva,' he said, 'you're not doing anything. Could you edit this letter?'

'Derek!' I cried. 'I'm resting!' I didn't know it, but this was Strike One.

Two hours later I entered our study, and Derek had spread his papers all over my desk. Nothing more. Insignificant! But now – Strike Two. 'That's *my* desk!' I cried.

For ten days, I mourned over these two small incidents. They somehow tipped me over the edge. I read the Bible, wept private tears and read the Bible some more. 'God,' I cried, 'I can't take this anymore. In my first 30 years of life, every emotional boundary was mowed down. I was treated like a slave. I know I'm overreacting, but I can't go through something like this again.'

I loved Derek passionately, but I felt like I was perishing inside. To top it off, Derek didn't seem to notice. Strike Three. I ran out into the night and walked empty streets. I hadn't taken an umbrella and the cold winter drizzle mingled with my tears.

Finally, in the silence, I understood. The problem wasn't Derek, it was me. I had grown bitter towards God because of Derek's blindness towards my needs, angry with myself because I didn't know how to deal with it. Now I had a choice. These two newly opened potholes of bitterness and anger loomed large in front of me.

I stood there soaked to the skin, then out of the blue I knew God wanted my best. But it was me who would need to change, to do something about it. Just because I had been silenced in my youth, that didn't mean I still had no voice. How unreasonable for me to think that Derek could read my mind! God wanted me to speak, and now it was as good a time as any.

I hurried home and found Derek at his desk, his shoulders slumped, his Bible open on his knees. I sat down beside him, and we talked. He embraced me, his voice breaking with emotion. 'I love you,' he said, 'but I'm not God. I can't guess what you're feeling. You have to tell me, so I don't go stomping in like an elephant and hurt you.'

God, in his graciousness, revealed my potholes one by one. I had to be willing to accept that even though these were reactions to past pain and abuse, I now had a choice in how to move on. I could respond to God's double imperative, 'Build up, build up.' Like Jasmin, and many others, it was trusting God's promises, listening to them and believing them with my whole heart that closed up these potholes.

There is another promise. The Bible says, 'I instruct you in the way of wisdom and lead you along straight paths. When you walk, your steps will not be hampered; when you run, you will not stumble' (Proverbs 4:11–12). As we trust God, together, us with our contrite and lowly hearts, him with his wonderful and trustworthy promises, together we can close those potholes.

Near the end of the Bible, God spoke to a church who had gone through hard times. He first acknowledged the incredible suffering she had endured, and then he comforted her, 'Do not be afraid' (Revelation 2:10). But he didn't stop there. He called out to her, 'Be faithful, even to the point of death, and I will give you life as your victor's crown.' As we walk with a contrite and lowly heart towards God, trusting in who he is, he will enable us to walk our road in life.

Yes, we will encounter situations where it will feel like death, potholes that would otherwise engulf us. But with God, as we journey with a willing heart, he gives us our own lives as a crown. *We will live*, not just as survivors, but as ones who thrive.

A time to reflect

Take some time to ponder this verse: 'I instruct you in the way of wisdom and lead you along straight paths. When you walk, your steps will not be hampered; when you run, you will not stumble' (Proverbs 4:11–12). Answer the following questions:

- What about this promise gives you hope?
- Which potholes does it fill up within your life?
- How could following God with a willing heart help you today?

If you would like, think about these verses later. Write down your thoughts in your journal.

6

GOD'S SIXTH CALL:
PASS THROUGH!

Pass through, pass through the gates! Prepare the way for the people.
Isaiah 62:10

God gives Jerusalem the confidence to step back into the world as a new person. And he gives us the confidence to be our new selves.

Pass through: can I do it?

Pass through, pass through the gates! Prepare the way for the people.

Much has already happened, and believe it or not, God has finished mending our hearts. But as with every grief and metaphorical meteor strike, it still takes time to rebuild our emotional, spiritual and relational strength. So, the final two double imperatives help solidify our healing.

Until now God has kept the focus on us, on our hearts, on enabling us to know and trust him. Now, he wants us to take our beautiful hearts and leave the security he has built around us. He wants us to step out into the world and gain mobility. But do we have the confidence that we are ready to go? Can we trust him that we have it in us to step out well?

God's last two double imperatives to Jerusalem call out, 'Pass through, pass through the gates! Prepare the way for the people. Build up, build up the highway! Remove the stones. Raise a banner for the nations' (Isaiah 62:10). And both are in one single verse! The first one called for Jerusalem to come out of seclusion and become visible, to come out of God's heart-hospital and into a world of broken hearts. He called her to pass through the gates. He calls us to do the same.

So often, after God has mended us, our inner world having been rewritten, we come out not knowing how we should re-engage with the world. We have a precious identity in God, but the world doesn't know us. We stand at the gate, looking out and ask a perplexed question, 'How do I fit in?'

It is a disconcerting question. God recognises this, yet he still asks us to pass through. As we do, he will lead us as he has in the past, through listening and trusting in him. Each tentative step will reinforce the healing he has done in us. Why? Because God knows when we are ready to go.

For me, I took a tentative step when I turned 27. Despite what I had been through, by then I had discovered how much God loved me. He had comforted me, woken me up and dressed me. He had worked in my heart so I could depart from fear. I had begun to trust God and knew he had my best interests at heart. But when I began to feel God's gentle nudge to step out and be me, there was someone who couldn't accept that I had changed. They couldn't let go of who I had been in the past. They liked that I had always backed down and always maintained a peace at all costs. They liked the control this let them have over me.

In retrospect, I shouldn't have cared about what this person thought; I should have taken the initiative to accept an invitation to go to a prayer meeting. God had healed my heart. But I didn't want to upset this person. I didn't want to get into a fight over something that in the big scheme of things seemed insignificant. But each little step we take out into the world, into being who we are, is important. I made a choice – a stinking choice. I voluntarily backed away and rang my friends to say I wasn't coming. How I cried on the phone, because I knew it was wrong, but at that moment it felt the easier choice.

The consequences? I hit an emotional crisis like I had never experienced before. A metaphorical meteor of my own engineering careered towards me, knocking me down. I had let God down. I had let myself down. And all that work of years gone by, I simply negated by one small act. I hadn't followed God into the freedom he had meant for me. I had refused to step out into the world and be me.

How I grieved. And even though, in retrospect, I still could have stepped out, it didn't occur to me. As far as I was concerned, if I could fail in this smallest of steps, I would never find the strength to get up and go. I still was weak, and to dream that I had strength was a delusion of grandeur.

So, I read my Bible and cried. But even here, God comforted me. He brought me to verses in the Bible and I began to wake up to an even deeper level of his love for me.

God wanted me to get back on my feet. He wanted me to do what I knew was right. He hadn't given up on me and neither should I. He had already given the strength and courage, I just needed to choose whose truth I believed – this person's or God's. But I didn't know how to retake this first little step, for my fragile self-confidence had evaporated.

This is where I began to realise my fault. It wasn't about confidence in myself, but my confidence in God. It wasn't about becoming independent of God as I stepped out, or standing alone in this world; it was about doing it together with God. The Bible said, 'Be strong in the Lord and in his mighty power' (Ephesians 6:10). It was about going with God. It was about doing things his way, for he had made me and knew me.

Then a thought came to mind… What if, because of my avoidance of conflict, I had stifled the emotions God gave me? They had atrophied and needed rebuilding. If God intended for me to be strong, this required exercising what was weak in my life, just like an atrophied muscle. I could exercise my emotions and make them strong once again. But I had no idea what to do, so I prayed to God. I would do this with him.

First, a basic truth came to mind – I was God's daughter. I didn't need to live like an emotional wreck. I didn't need to walk around always looking down, trying to hide so no one could see me. Instead, I had a dignified and wonderful identity. I could stand up with confidence because I was a daughter of the King of heaven. I could actually lift my head and look straight ahead because I belonged to him.

It took me a while, because it meant that I had to start valuing myself as God did. I had to see myself through his eyes, not the eyes of those who didn't want me to change. When I finally did take the brave step to lift my chin, to look life straight in the face, how I rejoiced.

Next, I remembered how God had already clothed me with strength. It took me more time, but I purposefully put a spring back into my step, and that bounce filled me with renewed courage. Then I relearned to breathe deep and slow, no longer those shallow breaths of fear and grief. It was as if God filled me with his life-giving breath, just like he had done when he created Adam and Eve. He was enabling me to live.

Yet my heart still hurt, and I protected it all day long by keeping my arms folded across my chest. It felt like a final protection from a world that kept hurting me. But, when I considered dropping my arms, I choked up with fear. Then I read a Bible verse, as if for the first time: 'Peace I leave with you; my peace I give you. I do not give to you as the world gives. Do not let your hearts be troubled and do not be afraid' (John 14:27). God wanted me to step out of this final pothole of fear. He wanted me to walk with him through the gate in a way I never dreamed of before. Even though my circumstances hadn't changed, I didn't have to live like a prisoner anymore. I let my arms drop. I let them hang there and entrusted my heart to God. Then together I stepped up to the threshold with God.

Sure, I still endured accusations and mocking, but I began to understand in a profound way that these didn't have to shape me. I could stand there looking out, secure in God that this new me would fit into this world, that I could walk away from lies. So, when a school leader approached me out of the blue and offered me a job as a teacher, I accepted. As I prepared my classroom for the first day, I stapled a single huge red question mark up on to the yellow bulletin board. With God's help, I would also enable my students to step out with the same competence and confidence in life. I would pray for them, that God would give them the freedom to live, the emotional strength to do what was right.

God isn't joking when he asks us to pass through those gates, to become visible in this world. Sure, we were turned inside out by the metaphorical meteors in our lives, and we changed, but God put us back together the way he always intended. In every new trouble we experience, in every subsequent healing of our hearts, God wants to be with us as we take a first step out.

It is that 'ta da!' moment. And it happened to Jerusalem. God made 'proclamation to the ends of the earth: "Say to Daughter Zion, 'See, your Saviour comes! See, his reward is with him, and his recompense accompanies him'"' (Isaiah 62:11). Everyone had their eyes on her. Everyone knew that God had done amazing things in her life. There was no hiding the fact. The same is true for us. Yet there is a wonderful twist. It isn't just for our sake, but for others as well.

Peter, one of Jesus' disciples, discovered this when King Herod arrested him for simply loving Jesus. He threw Peter into prison and put 16 soldiers on guard duty just in case he escaped. But the night before Peter's trial, as he slept between two soldiers, bound by chains and with sentries at the entrance, he too stepped out. 'Suddenly an angel of the Lord appeared… He struck Peter on the side and woke him up. "Quick, get up!" he said, and the chains fell off Peter's wrists. Then the angel said to him, "Put on your clothes and sandals… Wrap your cloak round you and follow me"' (Acts 12:7–8).

Amazing! The angel gave Peter the same instructions as God gave to Jerusalem. 'Get up. Get dressed. It's time to depart this awful prison.' Peter suddenly had a choice. He could doubt his eyes and ears because these things simply didn't happen. After all, some of his friends had already been killed. Or he could take a first step in his heart. Thankfully, he did, and it became a real step in real life.

The Bible tells us that 'they passed the first and second guards and came to the iron gate leading to the city. It opened for them by itself, and they went through it' (Acts 12:10). Suddenly, with Peter's decision to listen to the angel and follow him, he found himself freed. But the angel didn't leave him by the gate so that the guards could catch him and drag him back. The angel led him down the length of a street and then disappeared.

Peter stood there, confused, but then he 'came to himself and said, "Now I know without a doubt that the Lord has sent his angel and rescued me"' (Acts 12:11). And when this dawned on him, he knew just where to go, to his friend's house, to comfort those there, to help them step from grief to joy.

God is with us as we step out. Like Peter, he will lead us to those who also need comfort and help to step out.

I once met a woman at a community centre. I was there with my toddler, playing with toys in the children's corner, and as I looked up, our eyes met. She headed towards me, but people moved out of her way, as if she was somehow contaminated. 'May I join you?' she finally asked me.

I nodded and she sat in a child's chair opposite, a respectable distance from me. I smiled. 'I'm new in town,' I said. 'Have you lived here long?'

She didn't smile. 'All my life. My parents are buried around the corner. I have no brothers and sisters. Five years ago, my husband disappeared. I sent out a private investigator and they found him last year. I want to fly out and see if I can talk with him. Maybe I can win him back.'

Her frankness surprised me. 'That's really brave. I hope it goes well. When will you go?'

'I don't know,' she said. 'I don't know if I can get a ticket.'

'I don't understand.'

The woman explained the after-effects of a dangerous disease. Then she smiled, a sad sort of smile. 'The doctor says I only have a short time to live. Oh, how I wanted to have children.'

When I reacted, this woman smiled. 'It's okay. God promised he would heal me. Even if it is only in heaven, I am content. God always keeps his promises, but not always the way we expect.'

She paused and looked at my toddler. 'May I play with your baby?' she asked. 'The doctor says I'm not contagious. Your baby will be safe.'

I felt like gathering up my child and running away, even though I knew she was telling the truth. Yet suddenly I understood what I had to do. I stepped through a gate, one where I cared for someone outside my private world. I nodded.

She instantly slid to the floor and sat beside my toddler. She built a tower with blocks and made a spinning top go. My little one laughed. She laughed. Then she stood up. I stood up too. I threw my arms around her and gave her a hug. Her body slumped against mine, as if remembering human touch, for others too had rejected her. Tears sparkled in her eyes as she drew away. 'Thank you,' she whispered and left.

I never saw that woman again. When I asked about her at the community centre three weeks later, they said, 'Oh! She's gone. Went to find her husband three weeks ago...'

This woman knew who she was. She had God, and he had sustained her all along, but she needed help from others. And one of those things was my hug, from my own stepping out without fear. She finally saw how she fit in, and in which direction she should go. She found the courage to meet up with her husband, and this step brought admiration from those around.

David wrote a psalm about his feelings of being hated, hunted and the object of King Saul's rage. But he also wrote of the gracious God who saved him. 'I cry out to God Most High, to God, who vindicates me. He sends from heaven and saves me, rebuking those who hotly pursue me – God sends forth his love and his faithfulness' (Psalm 57:2–3). God helped David in an impossible situation. And because David personally dared to step out in a unique way, by writing a poem about his experience, by sharing it with others, his words have encouraged millions of us over the years.

A friend once told me, 'I know this sounds harsh, but God gave you a crash course. You wouldn't be the person you are, and come to it so quickly, if it hadn't been for all your troubles.'

Then she made a statement which gave me a new perspective as I stepped through the gate. 'God didn't take the thing which was designed for evil and make it good. He designed that the evil thing would be for the good. He is always at work to turn what is meant to harm us to bring us out into the light.' And her message enabled me to see God's bigger picture in my life. It helped me take a step towards reconciling with my past, knowing that God was bigger than every pain and grief I experienced.

Her message is for all of us. Despite every grief we experience, we can step through the gates after each one of them. We can fit into the plan God has for us. We can tell the world that good prevails, that light shines in darkness, that we can get up after every metaphorical meteor strike.

God asks us to pass through the gate and for each one of us it will be different. We will fit into this world in our own unique way. The help he sends us will vary. Yet there is one constant. As we read the Bible, we can always find God's comfort, his guidance. We can find his love. For God says, 'I know the plans I have for you… plans to prosper you and not to harm you, plans to give you hope and a future' (Jeremiah 29:11). And what God says matters.

God's double imperative to 'Pass through, pass through,' will always remain a challenge. We might long to see God's big picture beforehand and know every detail of our lives, but God encourages us to go forward with confidence, one step at a time. He will show us how we fit in. He will show us the way, despite the obstacles by the gate. And the very same promise God gave David, can be just as true for us: 'I will clothe his enemies with shame, but his head shall be adorned with a radiant crown' (Psalm 132:18). We can step around anything and anyone who would stop us passing through, and as we listen to God and accept his help, he enables us to shine. He enables us to laugh.

A time to reflect

Take some more time to think about the first part of Isaiah 62:10, 'Pass through, pass through the gates!' And if you would like, think about the following questions:

- Is there an area of your life where you would like to step out? What is holding you back?
- Is there something, someone, or a Bible verse that is giving you the courage to pass through the gate?
- How can God's double imperative give you the confidence to help another?

If you would like, pray about other areas in your life where you feel held back. Pray for God to send you the help needed to take a next step. Write down your prayers in your journal.

Pass through:
do I have to wait?

Pass through, pass through the gates! Prepare the way for the people.

There will be times after certain griefs that when we pass through the gates, ready to re-engage, God is silent. We wait, looking around. We wait some more. We anxiously cry out our own double imperative, 'Lord, speak to me! Please, *speak to me*! I can't just stand here and do nothing!' Oh, I have been there often enough.

We feel as if God has forgotten about us. Then we conjecture that maybe he actually wants us to take it from here. He wants us to figure it out ourselves. So, we look around and take stock. We evaluate the pros and cons. Then we get going.

We aren't alone in these feelings. The disciples felt like this after Jesus died and rose again. They received instructions to go to Galilee to meet Jesus, and they probably just about ran the whole way. But when they got there, he wasn't anywhere. They kicked their heels and waited. They hunted for him.

Then Peter, once a fisherman, made a statement to the other disciples that has resonated with me over the years: '"I'm going out to fish," Simon Peter told them, and they said, "We'll go with you." So they went out and got into the boat, but that night they caught nothing' (John 21). Peter had no idea what to do, so he did what he knew.

He and his friends worked hard all night but ended up with nothing to show for it. (And in some ways, that is what we expect when we go without Jesus.) But then someone appeared on the shore and called out. 'Throw your net on the right side of the boat and you will find some' (John 21:6). And for some reason they listened, catching so many fish they couldn't even haul it in.

Peter finally recognised who that person was. 'It is the Lord,' he cried out. Jesus had finally appeared. Yet, it is what we don't read that has surprised and encouraged me. Jesus didn't scold his disciples, saying, 'You've ruined things again. After everything I taught you over the last three years, you still run off on your own.'

Instead, he blessed them in their work. The net 'was full of large fish, 153, but even with so many fish the net was not torn' (John 21:11). He even had a little fire burning on the shore, with fish and bread cooking on it. He invited them to sit with him and share his meal. And those disciples, exhausted as they were, embraced the moment totally. Sure, they were weary, confused, hurting and feeling lost, but Jesus gave them what they needed. And what an encouragement that is for us.

Waiting is one of the hardest things to do. Oh, how I know. Because, what I desire from God might never happen. What I hope he will do might turn out differently. But God sees the bigger picture.

I experienced this when someone set about to cause me great distress, going around telling others how horrible I was. This woman even rallied numbers of people to her side and those people caught their breath when they saw me. They turned their backs on me and walked away.

I knew that I was in no way perfect, and that this woman and I had a differing set of values, but how I cried. And even though an elderly person told me this woman's actions stemmed from envy, and it wasn't my problem, it still was. The gossip kept spreading and it went on for years. And I couldn't stop it, and believe me, I did try.

After 25 years I had finally come to a point of trusting that God was the one who held my reputation in his hands. Then I happened to meet one of those people who avoided me. I had my children with me, and this lady watched how I related with them, how they loved me and the tenderness between us. She let out another gasp, a different kind, and said, 'What I was told, and what I am now seeing, doesn't compare. I believed every word and didn't think to check the facts. I am so sorry.'

I smiled a sad sort of smile and nodded. There was nothing else to say. Finally, I had regained a relationship. Yet it was more than just a reconciliation, for this woman saw goodness where she expected evil. She saw how she had been misled and could now turn away.

God's sixth double imperative to Jerusalem, 'Pass through, pass through the gates! Prepare the way for the people' (Isaiah 62:10) is followed by another verse. God told her, 'You will be called Sought After, the City No Longer Deserted' (Isaiah 62:12), and this took time to be revealed. Just as God presented her at the right time, so too he has a right time for us. For me, it took 25 years, but it was worth the wait.

Yet in all the time that I waited, God never condemned me for trying to patch up relationships. He never scolded me for shedding tears. Instead, he sent me verses telling me how much he loved me and how precious I was. He comforted me, woke me up and opened my eyes to the fact that only he can change hearts. He gave me strength and courage... and all of this just by the gate. For God knows that the lessons we learned in the first five double imperatives are lessons for life.

In some ways, we could compare ourselves to a six-year-old boy who after a bedtime story went to sleep in his bunkbed upstairs. But suddenly, in the night a loud thump filled the house. Then a wail. His mother ran into his room thinking he had fallen out of the top bunk in his sleep. She bent down to scoop him up off the floor. 'Are you hurt?' she asked.

'No!' he sobbed, annoyance in his voice. 'I want to fly. I jumped out of bed and flapped my arms. Why can't I fly?' He paused for a moment, and then looked up into his mother's face. 'I know what,' he said, brushing tears away. 'I'll jump from the top of the stairs. It will give me more time to flap.'

His mother gasped. 'I don't think that's a good idea,' she said. 'You might get hurt.' But her son refused to back down.

In the end she took him downstairs to talk with his father who was up late working in his study. The first thing he did was hug his son. He listened to the new plan his son had formed and said, 'Every time you want to jump, call me. I'll stand at the bottom and catch you. I don't want you to get hurt.'

'Let's go now, Daddy,' the young boy said. He ran to the stairs and climbed up a few steps. He jumped and his father caught him. He climbed up again, a few steps higher. Again, he jumped, and his father caught him. Then he climbed to the very top.

His mother cried out for him to stop, but it was too late. Her little boy had already jumped. He sailed through the air like a parachute jumper. His father stood at the bottom, his arms outstretched, his legs braced. 'This might hurt,' he whispered. But he was there for his son, encouraging a young boy as he worked through a new reality, and it became blessed as they spent time together.

God knows how we want to fly in life, but as we pass through the gate and into the world, the delays we experience give us time to accept our new realities. It takes time to work through our fears and frustrations. For just as this little boy listened to his father and trusted his solution, so can we. God wants to help us pass through that gate, and he will take the time that is needed to help us step out well. Sometimes, in certain situations, it takes a long time. For 'the Lord is not slow in keeping his promise, as some understand slowness. Instead he is patient with you, not wanting anyone to perish, but everyone to come to repentance' (2 Peter 3:9).

My friend, Alice, experienced this as well.

When my husband died twelve years ago, he left me with two small children. Even now, on one level, I still haven't figured out how to cope with the loneliness. I don't have any simple answers. There is a constant dull ache in my heart, and sometimes it gets sharper. Yet God comforts me all the time. I take a deep breath and remember... I am not on my own. He provides me with everything I need. So, I ask him to open my eyes to see how he is comforting me. I put on music or go for a walk. It could be a breeze caressing my face or the warmth of the sun. It could be a surprise visit or a pleasant email from a friend.

On another level, loneliness is an ongoing journey. As my children grow older and situations change, loneliness hits me in fresh ways. It doesn't happen very often, but it is still acute. Yet this one thing I know, God is my friend, my lover, my constant source of encouragement. He gives me what I need. But sometimes it isn't the kind of comfort I like. I want a pat on the back, and God gives me a prod. He does this because he loves me. He is with me.

Alice still mentions this loneliness even twelve years on, and still God lets her stay there at the gate. Even though she has gone through the seven double imperatives in her life, in this one area she still wonders what God has for her. But as a result, God has blessed her in her waiting, and he has become her friend, her lover. He stands with her.

For each one of us, as we listen to God's sixth call to 'Pass through, pass through the gate,' we are just as safe as when we were in his heart-hospital. We are just as loved. For 'The Lord will keep you from all harm – he will watch over your life; the Lord will watch over your coming and going both now and forevermore' (Psalm 121:7–8). And as others see us shining in our times of waiting, it will give them hope.

But what if we lose hope in the waiting? Again, we can look at Jesus' disciples. One evening, Jesus climbed into a boat with them as they planned to cross the sea. He was tired and lay down on a cushion in the stern. He fell asleep. Suddenly, 'a furious squall came up, and the waves broke over the boat, so that it was nearly swamped' (Mark 4:37), but the disciples didn't wake him.

Alone, they watched the waves crash in. They watched the boat sink lower and lower into the sea. They watched the water level rise in the boat, and still they didn't ask for help. It wasn't until they were ready to submerge, and they couldn't bear it anymore, that 'the disciples woke him and said to him, "Teacher, don't you care if we drown?"' (Mark 4:38).

Jesus woke up and stilled the waves, but then he asked his disciples, 'Why are you so afraid? Do you still have no faith?' (Mark 4:40).

In our desperate waiting, Jesus is with us. It might feel like he is asleep. It might feel like he is absent, but he is with us, and he stills the storms in our hearts. For waiting at the gate, waiting for Jesus to take us the next step, takes just as much faith. The Bible says, 'Blessed is the one who perseveres under trial because, having stood the test, that person will receive the crown of life that the Lord has promised to those who love him' (James 1:12). As we hang on in there, we receive yet another crown – life. For in our waiting, we still live. And in our at-long-last entry into the world, we bring our lives, a testimony to a wonderful and living God.

A time to reflect

Take a few moments to think about Psalm 121:7–8 again: 'The Lord will keep you from all harm – he will watch over your life; the Lord will watch over your coming and going both now and forevermore.' If you would like, consider the following questions.

- Is there an area in your life where God seems to have forgotten you? What is it?
- How do these verses encourage you as you wait?
- What about God enables you to see a blessing as you wait?

If you would like, take a moment to record what God is teaching you in this time of waiting. Write about it in your journal and if you feel able, share it with someone else.

7

GOD'S SEVENTH CALL:
BUILD UP!

Build up, build up the highway! Remove the stones. Raise a banner for the nations.
Isaiah 62:10

Like Jerusalem, God wants us to share his seven calls, enabling others to draw close to him. And as we do, our hearts will grow in confidence.

Build up: can I forgive?

Build up, build up the highway! Remove the stones. Raise a banner for the nations.

God's final double imperative calls us to step away from the gate, away from shelter and into the wind of the world. As we finally step out, he calls us to, 'Build up, build up the highway! Remove the stones. Raise a banner for the nations' (Isaiah 62:10). But you might be saying, 'Haven't we already done this? Road building came in God's fifth call!' And then you quote the verse to me. 'Build up, build up, prepare the road! Remove the obstacles out of the way of my people' (Isaiah 57:14).

You are right, but the fifth one focused on us, removing the obstacles from our lives. It was about our journey towards God. Now, God calls for us to lift our eyes to the nations, to others, to those who we encounter near and far. He asks us to inspect the road which leads to them, to fix it and raise a banner, an eye-catching flag which points to God.

Yet most often we will step out where we began our journey of heart-healing with God, into the situations and amid the people who hurt us. And just like Jerusalem, we will step directly into life. For our road building to the world begins where we are. And it is here that we are confronted with the costliest thing we will ever do: to forgive those who hurt us. In Luke 24:47 it says, 'Repentance for the forgiveness of sins will be preached in his name to all nations, beginning at Jerusalem.' Through Jerusalem's heart attitude and our own, we can build up that road.

My friend Becks shared her courageous story of building a road right where she was.

My mother had many expectations on how I should behave, what to like or dislike, and where I should excel. I don't know if they were projections or simply her wanting control, but whatever the case I shed many tears. Even as a child I realised the expectations were unrealistic. She never acknowledged that I was separate from her, and I thought that maybe I was crazy, just imagining all the problems.

My friends didn't make it any easier either. They told me to 'go and ditch her,' but I knew if I did, I would stop feeling. Then the Bible showed me how love and forgiveness should be my motivators, and how I shouldn't cling to self-preservation. I tried to take the initiative to build a bridge instead.

This meant I prepared myself for each conversation we had. I factored in that I might get hurt and disappointed. I discovered what I wanted and what to expect. I also decided to have a listening ear towards her. I tried to pray positively as well. 'Lord, please give me love. Give us memories and shared experiences which connect us.'

It was true that I couldn't add what was missing in our relationship, but it didn't have to be perfect either. Someday in heaven I knew it would be, and this gave me great hope. Yet I still find that sometimes I get thrown off, especially when I am hurt. I try to remember to not drag up old wounds. I try to remember she does love, even if partially.

Becks knew that God loves totally, that he cares completely and that no one can be excluded from his love. Yet for us, as we build a road to those who have hurt us, my friend Becks summed it up so well. She showed her beautiful love by forgiving her mother.

Yet it comes with a caution, as Jasmin once said.

I have learned how there is a danger when I approach someone who has hurt me. If they turn it around and rebuff me instead, it will actually make me physically ill. I have heard it happen to others as well. I myself developed a digestive condition when I was unfairly treated. This condition still flares up every time I feel stress.

I have also found that the biggest problem in trying to resolve a conflict is that the person who hurts me may be incapable of understanding what they did. I may never be reconciled in that relationship, but it doesn't mean I can't be free. I can still forgive them, even though they will never acknowledge it. I can let go of them and get on with my life.

It is a caution to remember, and thankfully it doesn't mean that we can't forgive. As my friend said, we can let go and get on with our lives. But I have found forgiveness a fragile process, and it is something I have struggled with for years, especially when hurtful situations are still ongoing. Of all the double imperatives, building up a road towards those who have deeply hurt me has been one of the costliest.

At first, I didn't even know where to begin, so I spent time reading about Jesus, my hero, my role model. How did he deal with those who hurt him profoundly, especially when his enemies betrayed, tortured and murdered him? Then I read about when he hung on the cross and he said something that finally helped me take the first step: 'Father, forgive them' (Luke 23:34).

So, this is what I prayed. 'Father, I don't know how to forgive, but please would you forgive them for me.' And at that point, it was enough. I could rest in the fact that at least someone had forgiven them.

Several years later, God took me to the second part of that verse, 'Father, forgive them, for they do not know what they are doing.' I began look-ing into the hearts of those who hurt me. Some of them had no idea of the carnage they were causing, and if they had fully grasped how every person on earth has profound dignity and worth, they would never have treated me like that. But they didn't, because I never told them. I hinted here and there, but never just said, 'Excuse me, you are hurting me. This is unacceptable.'

Yet even here timing was important. Concerning the person who maligned me for years, who destroyed various of my relationships, I wanted to scream so this person could hear the volume of my pain. I wanted to demand justice with a volley of sledgehammer-like words. But as I prayed, I read a verse which surprised and guided me, Joshua 6:10: 'Do not give a war cry, do not raise your voices, do not say a word until the day I tell you to shout. Then shout!' I felt I should remain silent until God released me. For 15 years I didn't say a word. Then suddenly one day I felt released.

I wrote a letter straight away, but still with a sledgehammer attitude throughout. I wanted that person to understand my continued pain. But, before I sent it, I showed it to Derek, as a check on my heart. He shook his head.

For the next nine years I wrote a letter once a year, and Derek shook his head each time. Yes, I grew frustrated because I knew I still wanted to hurt back, word for word, tear for tear. But on the tenth year, it finally didn't matter. Even if this person kept on hurting, it didn't have to affect my day-to-day living. It only robbed me of joy when I let it. And if those others who had abandoned me still chose to believe this person's lies, that was their problem, not mine. It wasn't my duty to re-educate them.

My heart changed when I realised how God loved this person so intensely. So, I sent yet another letter and asked if we could meet face to face. This person replied, 'If you had sent this letter even a month earlier, I would have dismissed everything you said. In the last two weeks God has been showing me a lot of things about my life…' I wept.

This person and I began a tentative acquaintanceship with honesty and respect. We spent time clearing out potholes, building up a road. It was never perfect, and we never became bosom buddies, but God could come into our relationship. And as we talked, this person began sharing about taking steps to forgive her parents, friends and me for not fulfilling plans she felt God had given her for us. She said something like this:

I have learned that whenever someone hurts me, it is as if they go into debt to me, and I inevitably demand them to pay up. I demand their respect, for them to stop doing what they are doing, and I absolutely demand an apology. But most people who hurt me will never see it my way, so I am left with an unresolved problem. They owe me an enormous debt and I want my payment.

> I have two choices, to keep demanding of them what they will
> never give or release them from their debt. If I release them,
> I release myself. I don't need their respect. My well-being isn't
> tied up in their apology. I am free to move on in life, because
> I don't have this huge debt to collect. God is the one who gives
> me what I need.

How my heart resonated with her words. How it clarified my understanding and became the road-building material towards this person.
For God calls out to each one of us, 'In the wilderness prepare the way
for the Lord; make straight in the desert a highway for our God... The
glory of the Lord will be revealed and all people will see it together'
(Isaiah 40:3, 5). And as we mend the road between ourselves and others, it becomes a road towards God.

God will help us build each road well, and in a way which will enable
people to find him. Yet we can grow discouraged if others ignore what
we have worked so hard to mend. But we must keep remembering that
our job is to give our time and effort to build, not make people walk
those roads. God is the one who will help each person along, enabling
them at their right time.

At the end of Isaiah, God continued speaking to Jerusalem, lifting her
horizons to the nations. He said, 'They will proclaim my glory among
the nations. And they will bring all your people, from all the nations, to
my holy mountain in Jerusalem as an offering to the Lord – on horses,
in chariots and wagons, and on mules and camels' (Isaiah 66:19–20).
Jerusalem took the incredibly brave step to reach out to the nations with
whom she had been unfaithful, to those who had destroyed her. She
told them about her wonderful God, the one who truly loves and cares.

King David did the same. He too had been deeply hurt, but he could
still give a message to those around him. He said, 'Sing the praises
of the Lord, enthroned in Zion; proclaim among the nations what he
has done' (Psalm 9:11). David built up roads by declaring what God

had done in his life, by showing that no gate, no passion or pothole, no fear can stop God from loving us. And his words encourage us to share God's heart to anyone who will listen.

The apostle Paul did the same. In 2 Corinthians 11:23–33, he lists the things which happened to him: prison; floggings; stoning; shipwreck; bandits; hunger; nakedness. And still he could write, 'Praise be to the God and Father of our Lord Jesus Christ, the Father of compassion and the God of all comfort' (2 Corinthians 1:3). God had held him together with his tender care.

Paul could look beyond his troubles and consider the grief of others. He could see that God is the one 'who comforts us in all our troubles, so that we can comfort those in any trouble with the comfort we ourselves receive from God' (2 Corinthians 1:4). For just as God had comforted him, Paul could reach out and give this comfort to others. He could build roads to those around him because of the road God had built with him.

But what of the flip side? What if we have been the ones who hurt others? Maybe we didn't mean to, or maybe we did, but if we continue talking about God's goodness and are at the same time unkind to others, those people we've hurt will turn away from us. For what we do will cause pain and offence.

I have done it often enough, becoming a pothole in another person's life. But even here, God is gracious in his fairness. As I accept my responsibility in hurting another, as I ask forgiveness and make amends as best as I can, I can begin my road building once again. And even though it might take years for it all to work out, God will help me every step of the way.

None of us is perfect. We will make mistakes. We will hurt others. But as we build with a contrite and humble attitude towards God and those around us, we will begin to see God at work. And even if those we have offended choose not to forgive us, Jesus still washes us clean and restores our hearts. He enables us to walk in continued reaching-out love without self-recrimination and shame.

Our lives will touch those around us, and as they see us grappling to be our best with God, they might just turn to him. They might hurry down the road we are building and find our glorious God as well. And then our joy will resonate with that of the apostle Paul: 'For what is our hope, our joy, or the crown in which we will glory in the presence of our Lord Jesus when he comes? Is it not you?' (1 Thessalonians 2:19). For each one of us, no matter our past, can give our all to building up roads for God. While we might never know the smallest part of our influence on others, we can rest assured that in heaven we will. There is a crown for us.

A time to reflect

Take a few moments to think on these verses: 'Praise be to the God and Father of our Lord Jesus Christ, the Father of compassion and the God of all comfort, who comforts us in all our troubles, so that we can comfort those in any trouble with the comfort we ourselves receive from God' (2 Corinthians 1:3–4). If you feel able, consider the following questions below:

- How do you think God's comfort enables you to forgive? To ask for forgiveness?
- How is the comfort you have received from God enough to help anyone in any kind of trouble?
- Take some time to think about your relationships. What can you give of yourself in building up a road towards them?

Record your thoughts in your journal and if you feel able, pray for these people.

Build up:
what of those walls?

Build up, build up the highway! Remove the stones. Raise a banner for the nations.

Just because God calls us to 'build up, build up the highway! Remove the stones. Raise a banner for the nations' (Isaiah 62:10), doesn't mean people will listen. Sometimes people have their own reasons for blocking out God.

Derek and I visited a very elderly lady one Saturday afternoon, but I couldn't shake a sense of sadness. This lady had everything she wanted. She lived in a manor house which had been converted into the poshest of residential homes. She served us a proper tea from china cups and delicate cakes with silver cutlery. She smiled and made small talk.

I so wanted to bring up the subject, allude to God in some way, but she had made it clear in the past how she had no interest at all. I tried to find a chink in the conversation, to insert a thought or two, but she manoeuvred the conversation with great skill. So Derek and I bid this lady goodbye and headed towards our car. But I suddenly stopped. 'Derek,' I said, 'I have to go back. Wait for me.'

I hurried to her apartment and found this woman still sitting on her tapestried armchair, by her velvet curtains, looking out a stone-arched window into an ancient garden. I fell on my knees before her. 'Please, may I pray with you?'

She looked down at me, a bemused smile on her lips. 'No, my dear. That kind of a thing is for people like you. I don't need it.'

I nodded, stood up and kissed her on the cheek. The next day we heard that she had passed away, only a few hours after we left. Grief hit my heart. I loved this woman. Why did she find it so hard to come to God?

Even God encountered this when he tried to reason with his people. He said, 'Because you have rejected this message, relied on oppression and depended on deceit, this sin will become for you like a high wall, cracked and bulging, that collapses suddenly, in an instant' (Isaiah 30:12–13). My beloved elderly friend and God's people had decided to build up high walls, barriers to shield themselves from God. But what they didn't know – those walls would eventually fall.

One day I spotted a farmer rebuilding a broken-down stone wall, which only a few days earlier had reached up above my head. But now it lay in a pile in the grass. 'Hello!' I called. 'What makes a perfectly good wall collapse?'

The greying farmer straightened his back. He shuffled over to his pickup and leaned against it. 'There are several reasons,' he said, looking at the wall. 'This one was built a 150 years ago. See how it has a layer of stone on one side and on the other. See how the centre is filled with earth. It should have been filled with stone. Eventually the soil washes out and the wall collapses.'

I nodded, and the farmer glanced over at me, his brows knit together. He pointed to the wall again. 'This wall was also built with overburdened stone. That is stone which was picked up from the fields, where it had already been affected by rain and frost. It crumbles with time and the wall collapses. This wall should have been built with stone from the local mine.'

He kept on going. 'It could also have been children pulling stones out of the wall. But the most likely reason is the tractor I drive. The vibration will shake any wall apart. A normal eleven-ton tractor will do some damage, but when harvest comes, I drive a 30-ton tractor. Parts of the wall always come down then.' He smiled. 'Well, it's back to work.'

I thanked the farmer and ambled on. Those walls really did resemble the barriers people throw up in their lives; they get thrown up in a hurry to hide themselves from God, but life has a way of wearing those walls down. It could be the tiniest thing or a whopping 30-ton problem. Eventually they collapse, no matter how much a person might want to avoid God. And because we too may have experienced this in our lives, and we have seen how God helped us step out from behind the barriers we once built, we can reach out to others with deep compassion.

God is love and love doesn't give up. And even though walls will get hastily built up on every side, God says, 'I revealed myself to those who did not ask for me; I was found by those who did not seek me. To a nation that did not call on my name, I said, "Here am I, here am I"' (Isaiah 65:1). God raises his flag higher, so people can see it above their barricades, so they can know there is another way to live. He wants us to join him in waving his precious flag – Jesus. For it is through Jesus that we experience his comfort and hope, his courage and strength, his love. It is through Jesus that we can share this same message with those behind their barricades. The words God gave Isaiah are the same words Jesus used of himself:

> The Spirit of the Sovereign Lord is on me, because the Lord has anointed me to proclaim good news to the poor. He has sent me to bind up the broken-hearted, to proclaim freedom for the captives and release from darkness for the prisoners, to proclaim the year of the Lord's favour and the day of vengeance of our God, to comfort all who mourn.
> ISAIAH 61:1–2; see LUKE 4:18–19

We can declare Jesus' love to those hiding behind their walls. For when we grieved, we received Jesus' good news. When we were broken-hearted, he bandaged us. When we were captives in dark prisons, Jesus set us free, not to a selfish freedom to spend on ourselves, but a generous one to reach out to others. Jesus' call to build up the highway comes through his own words: 'My command is this: love each other as I have loved you. Greater love has no one than this: to lay down one's life for one's friends' (John 15:12–13). Every single thing he has put inside our hearts and lives, we can share with others.

From time to time, I hear these words from those who have come out of deep brokenness. They all say a similar thing. 'I can't believe it. Look at me! Look at what Jesus has done! I should be in the gutter or dead, but Jesus gave me life. He took all the mess and made it into something good. He gave me dignity. But he gave me something even more. He entrusted me to help others.' They laugh, and the joy on their faces is palpable. Jesus had helped them as they walked through unimaginable difficulties, and now they could give to others with amazing generosity. And as they did, often they were there when someone else's wall came crumbling down. They were there to help the broken-hearted.

All of us have a mission. For Jerusalem it was: 'I will extend peace to her like a river, and the wealth of nations like a flooding stream; you will feed and be carried on her arm and dandled on her knees' (Isaiah 66:12). Jerusalem would nourish the nations. She would build roads to them and feed them. And the same is true for us. We are called to pass on Jesus' love and the invitation that anyone can experience it, that anyone can be satisfied in him.

God, the one who gives hope, wants to show them that they too are worth his comfort. God, the one who gives courage and strength, wants them to wake up and get dressed. God, the one who enables, wants them to leave all other passions and have a precious relationship with him. And God asks us to step out for this, just as he asked his Son. For Jesus himself passed through the gates of heaven and is building roads in this world. Sure, on earth he encountered the formidable walls others had built, but it didn't stop him in his tracks.

Jesus also wants us to remember that this road building to the nations isn't hindered because of our own griefs in life, or because of those who still can't receive God's heart. For he said, 'In this world you will have trouble. But take heart! I have overcome the world' (John 16:33). For even amid the ongoing metaphorical meteor strikes in our lives, or the grief we might experience because of the high walls our loved ones have built, we can still show God's love.

Many years ago, when Derek and I began working with a charity, we moved to another city, but we didn't have enough money to make ends meet. Month in and month out, we barely scraped out an existence. Yet despite this, many people still came through our house. Thankfully, we had enough to serve a simple meal, but nothing more. How I wanted to give them a piece of chocolate at the end of each meal.

I asked God for a jar of chocolates, then shared my prayer with Derek. His eyes grew big. 'Eva, we have much greater needs at the moment! Anyway, God wouldn't answer a prayer like that because it isn't necessary.'

His words didn't deter me. By then I had learned through the hard knocks of life to never give up. I could trust my judgement and intuition. I could step through that gate and smile. I assured Derek that I also prayed for our living expenses, but this was something additional on my heart.

Two days later a neighbour dropped by. They brought over a huge jar of chocolates, the biggest one I had ever seen. I glanced over at Derek and grinned. His eyes went wide with astonishment. He laughed. Later he said, 'Well, I obviously got that one wrong. I sure have some rethinking to do about God.'

For the six years we worked with those people, that jar never went empty. No person ever lacked a chocolate. For as I shared this story with each new guest, without Derek and I knowing, they spread the news around and made it their mission to keep that jar full. And what could have become a barrier in my life, of being upset with God because we could barely make ends meet, became an opportunity to help others meet a God who comforts and loves. It also gave them the precious opportunity to participate in his love.

'Comfort, comfort, my people' (Isaiah 40:1–2) was God's first call to Jerusalem. It was a call not just for Jerusalem's ears, but for anyone who could rally around her, to anyone who cared. And as we gather around the hurting, speaking tenderly to them, giving comfort, they can also find God's crown of comfort.

And for us who have gone through God's seven double imperatives, let's continue hanging on to our own crowns of comfort in every metaphorical meteor strike and grief. For Jesus says, 'I am coming soon. Hold on to what you have, so that no one will take your crown' (Revelation 3:11). We are whole, and we can keep it that way, no matter what happens to us. For we are God's precious daughters.

A time to reflect

If you would like, take a moment to think back on God's seven double imperatives, for he has called each of us to:

- Accept his comfort.
- Wake up and look around.
- Get dressed in his strength and courage.
- Depart from anything which would hurt us.
- Build up a relationship with him in life.
- Pass through the gates and look at the world.
- Build up a road for others to find God.

As you have grown to know God, consider the following questions:
- How has God changed your life over the last few months?
- How has your view of yourself changed?
- How has this changed your perspective of God? Your perspective of Jesus? Your perspective of others?

If you are able, take some time to thank God. And as you think of the next step in your life, ask God to keep guiding you. This is the beginning of a lifelong journey with God's crown of comfort firmly on your head.

Notes

1. The double imperatives are in: Isaiah 40:1–2; 51:17; 52:1; 52:11; 57:14; 62:10a; and 62:10b. There is another place, Isaiah 55:2, where the NIV is the only Bible translation that translates this Hebrew text as a double imperative, 'Listen, listen.' As I went back to the original Hebrew, it became clear that the NIV stands alone here. For this reason, I have left it out. All other translations (as far as I can find, and I have checked over 50) say, 'Listen carefully', 'Hearken diligently' or a variation of these words.
2. Psalm 132:13. Here God calls Jerusalem, 'Zion'. He uses the two names interchangeably.
3. For the definition of 'comfort' in Isaiah 40:1, see **biblehub.com/ hebrew/5162.htm**.
4. P.A. Dunavold, 'Happiness, hope, and optimism', spring 1997, **csun.edu/~vcpsy00h/students/happy.htm**.
5. See Matthew 14:22–32.
6. For definitions of the Hebrew words translated 'salvation' and 'righteousness', see **biblehub.com/strongs/isaiah/61-10.htm**.
7. Baal – a god of war, which included child sacrifice.
8. A line from a hymn by Theodore Kitching, *War Cry* magazine, Salvation Army, 6 February 1915.

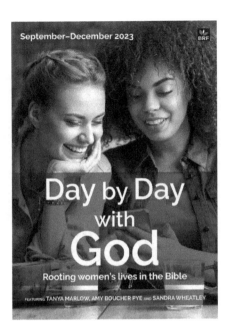

September–December 2023

BRF

Day by Day
with
God

Rooting women's lives in the Bible

FEATURING TANYA MARLOW, AMY BOUCHER PYE AND SANDRA WHEATLEY

Day by Day with God Bible reading notes are specifically written for women. All the contributors are women and write from a woman's perspective. The entries for each day contain a suggested Bible reading, with the key verse written out in full, a helpful comment that engages heart and mind and a short reflection or prayer. Whatever your current situation in life, you will be inspired and encouraged by these notes.

Day by Day with God
Rooting women's lives in the Bible
Published three times a year in January, May and September
Available in regular print and as an app for Android, iPhone and iPad

brfonline.org.uk

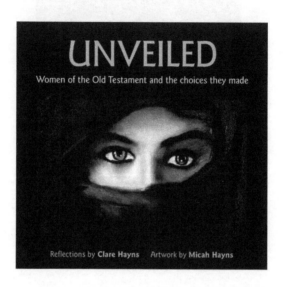

Some women of the Hebrew scriptures are well known, but many others are barely remembered. Even when they are, we often don't pause on them long enough to think about what we might learn from them. *Unveiled*, written with frankness and humour and illustrated with striking artwork from a young Oxford-based artist, explores the stories of 40 women in 40 days. Each reflection ends with a short application to everyday life, guidance for further thought and a prayer.

Unveiled
Women of the Old Testament and the choices they made
Clare Hayns; illustrated by Micah Hayns
978 1 80039 072 0 £12.99

brfonline.org.uk

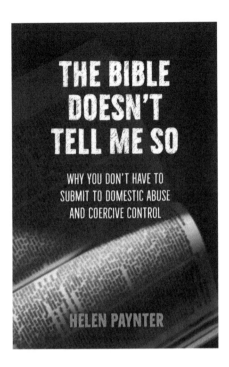

This book is addressed directly to women experiencing domestic abuse, and to those who seek to support them, including pastoral leaders, friends and support organisations. It debunks the myths – perpetuated by some abusers and, unwittingly, by many churches – which prevent women from getting out of harm's way. It helps them realise that the Bible does not belong to their abuser but is a text of liberation. Written with careful attention to pastoral issues, it closely examines and clearly explains the relevant scriptural texts.

The Bible Doesn't Tell Me So
Why you don't have to submit to domestic abuse and coercive control
Helen Paynter
978 0 85746 989 2 £8.99

brfonline.org.uk

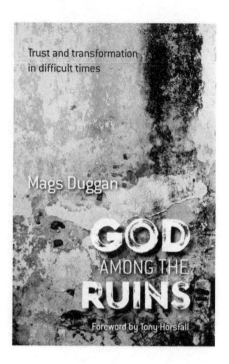

Where do we turn when our world is falling apart? It takes courage to hope; to stand in our confusion and grief and still to believe that 'God is not helpless among the ruins'. Guided by Habakkuk and his prophetic landmarks, we are drawn on a reflective journey through the tangled landscape of bewildered faith, through places of wrestling and waiting, and on into the growth space of deepened trust and transformation. As you read, discover for yourself the value and practice of honest prayer, of surrender, of silence and listening, and of irrepressible hoping.

God among the Ruins
Trust and transformation in difficult times
Mags Duggan
978 0 85746 575 7 £8.99

brfonline.org.uk